SAGE was founded in 1965 by Sara Miller McCune to support the dissemination of usable knowledge by publishing innovative and high-quality research and teaching content. Today, we publish over 900 journals, including those of more than 400 learned societies, more than 800 new books per year, and a growing range of library products including archives, data, case studies, reports, and video. SAGE remains majority-owned by our founder, and after Sara's lifetime will become owned by a charitable trust that secures our continued independence.

Los Angeles | London | New Delhi | Singapore | Washington DC | Melbourne

IN
FOREST,
FIELD
AND
FACTORY

Thank you for choosing a SAGE product!
If you have any comment, observation or feedback,
I would like to personally hear from you.

Please write to me at **contactceo@sagepub.in**

Vivek Mehra, Managing Director and CEO, SAGE India.

Bulk Sales

SAGE India offers special discounts
for purchase of books in bulk.
We also make available special imprints
and excerpts from our books on demand.

For orders and enquiries, write to us at

Marketing Department
SAGE Publications India Pvt Ltd
B1/I-1, Mohan Cooperative Industrial Area
Mathura Road, Post Bag 7
New Delhi 110044, India

E-mail us at **marketing@sagepub.in**

Subscribe to our mailing list
Write to **marketing@sagepub.in**

This book is also available as an e-book.

IN
FOREST,
FIELD
AND
FACTORY

Adivasi Habitations through Twentieth-Century India

GAURI BHARAT

Los Angeles | London | New Delhi
Singapore | Washington DC | Melbourne

Copyright © Gauri Bharat, 2019

All rights reserved. No part of this book may be reproduced or utilized in any form or by any means, electronic or mechanical, including photocopying, recording or by any information storage or retrieval system, without permission in writing from the publisher.

First published in 2019 by

SAGE Publications India Pvt Ltd
B1/I-1 Mohan Cooperative Industrial Area
Mathura Road, New Delhi 110 044, India
www.sagepub.in

SAGE Publications Inc
2455 Teller Road
Thousand Oaks, California 91320, USA

SAGE Publications Ltd
1 Oliver's Yard, 55 City Road
London EC1Y 1SP, United Kingdom

SAGE Publications Asia-Pacific Pte Ltd
18 Cross Street #10-10/11/12
China Square Central
Singapore 048423

YODA Press
79 Gulmohar Enclave
New Delhi 110049
www.yodapress.co.in

Published by Vivek Mehra for SAGE Publications India Pvt Ltd. Typeset in 10.5/13 pt Bembo by Fidus Design Pvt Ltd, Chandigarh.

Library of Congress Cataloging-in-Publication Data Available

ISBN: 978-93-5328-806-8 (HB)

SAGE YODA Team: Amrita Dutta, Vandana Gupta, Arpita Das, Ishita Gupta and Tanya Singh

Contents

List of Illustrations

TABLE

FIGURES

Acknowledgements

This book has its origins in my PhD research and I am deeply grateful to my supervisors Dr Daniel Rycroft and Prof. John Mack at the University of East Anglia, Norwich, United Kingdom, for their support, meticulous feedback and constant encouragement. They were a source of intellectual and emotional inspiration throughout this project. I would also like to thank the School of Art, Media and American Studies at UEA for scholarships that made this study possible. At the Faculty of Architecture, CEPT University, India, where I work, I particularly thank Dr Jigna Desai, Dr Rutul Joshi and Sankalpa, whose camaraderie and ready discussions were instrumental in shaping this project and helping me persevere with it. To Niyati Mehta, heartfelt thanks for crucial and timely advice on how and why this book may interest people. I would also like to send a shout-out to various academic colleagues who responded to this work during conferences and seminars and whose questions and comments have enriched the project.

In the fieldwork villages, I am indebted to Malti Hansdah, Bishwanath Hansdah, Anju Murmu, Meena Singh, Kausalya, Seluka and Ghasiramji, who let me into their homes and lives and patiently answered my questions. Their friendship was a source of support and made the fieldwork a fulfilling and memorable experience. I am grateful to Dr C. R. Sardar, P. C. Mahato, Binay Mahato and Lakhan Soren of the Tata Steel Rural Development Society for assistance during fieldwork and for introducing me to the villages.

I am particularly grateful to Prof. Asoka Kumar Sen, Dr Sadan Jha and Dr Krishna Gajjar for taking the time to share their comments on the work and suggestions with regard to its publication. My heartfelt thanks to Arpita Das of Yoda Press for being such an inspiring editor. Special thanks also goes to Ishita Gupta and the teams at Yoda Press and SAGE Publications for bringing this volume into being. I have learnt so much from all of you!

Finally, this thesis is dedicated to my families, without whose unstinting love and support, I could not have convinced of doing this project. My foster families in the UK, Laura Drysdale, Gaia Shaw, Dharini Ravi, Nadine Zubair, Emily Crane and Domenigo Sergi, whose conversations have stayed with me and continued to inspire me long after the completion of the PhD. To my parents-in-law, Mayuri and Pankaj Shah, who generously helped me follow and fulfil my dreams and willingly took care of my family during my absence. I am very grateful to them. To my aunt, Usha Rajagopalan, a big thanks for all the uplifting conversations about writing a book. My parents, R. Bharat and Vijaya Bharat, and sister Sheetal, who, apart from assistance and emotional support, prove to be an ideal for me to aspire to. To my husband, Priyank, and children, Nandana and Tanuj, who keep me grounded and whose love and affection is a buoy each and every day. I can never sufficiently express my gratitude to them.

There are many others whom I have interacted with and learnt something from during the two decades that this project has been in the making. As the book comes into fruition, I hope to personally let you know and thank you for helping me along the way. While I cannot name all the people here, I would like to say that it has been a privilege to have had the opportunity to pursue this work, and I thank every one of you for your love, help and support. However, any shortcoming in this work is my responsibility alone.

Introduction: Foregrounding Change

Jharkhand in eastern India is one of the oldest centres of industrialisation in South Asia while also being home to a large Adivasi (indigenous) population. The narrative of industrialisation has dominated life and history in this region and overshadowed the Adivasi hinterland that it developed within. As a young person growing up in Jamshedpur, which is one of the largest iron and steel producing centres in south Jharkhand, I was largely oblivious to the presence of Adivasis in the city and beyond. I had heard of them of course, but they were almost abstract, living somewhere deep within unknown forests, far outside the modernity of the city. Jamshedpur had, and continues to have, a very mixed population with diverse communities from all over India. I grew up in neighbourhoods with people from many different backgrounds, speaking many different languages. Most communities have cultural institutions as a marker of their presence within the city. Notable Adivasi institutions were, for the most part, missing. Except for weekly markets and a passing glance at crowds of Adivasi labourers outside factory gates, one did not encounter Adivasi culture and society within the public life of the city. Recognising this gap, during the final project for my undergraduate architecture degree, I decided to explore the interface between Adivasi communities and the city. The first potential site was a tribal cultural centre but it was a rather quiet institution with a few displays and events about and for Adivasi communities. The next and more complex site was the congregation of Adivasi labourers in market places and outside the factory gates in various parts of the city. Adivasi villagers and slum residents gathered at specific places each morning and prospective employers looking for *mistris* (brick layers, plasterers or painters) and *rejas* (women labourers who usually assisted the men) came to these sites with job offers. A host of allied activities such as small shops, vendors selling food and drink and various other knick-knacks sprung up around these locations. Such sites clearly belonged to both Adivasi and industrial worlds and presented an intriguing challenge to my own preconceived notions about Adivasis and their relationship to the city. Thus began my research into the culture, mobility, economy, landscape and architecture of Adivasi communities in and around Jamshedpur. Over the years, I realised that the social invisibility of Adivasis or the perception of their primitiveness was not a personal shortcoming alone, but a much wider social and historical construct that pervaded the popular perception of these communities in the urban centres of the region.

The popular history of Jamshedpur begins with the discovery of iron along the banks of the River Subarnarekha (literally meaning 'line of gold'). A local company gave form to this historical moment through a vivid televised advertisement and it became etched in popular memory.[1] The story described a young geologist who wrote of the presence of iron ore in the hills around the Subarnarekha. Meanwhile, Jamsetji Nasserwanji Tata, the pioneering industrialist who eventually established the steel plant and after whom the city of Jamshedpur is named, came to realise that the future of the country lay in economic independence through the development of industrialisation. The advertisement showed how he searched extensively for a site in eastern India where steel could be manufactured from iron ore and travelled to industrial centres in Manchester and in North America looking for the latest technologies. Following a letter from geologist P. N. Bose, who informed him about the rich mineral deposits in Sackhi in the Mayurbhanj state, Jamsetji sent across people who surveyed this thickly forested area on horseback. The metal of the horseshoe clinked against the soil, indicating the presence of iron ore. Combined with the availability of water and the proximity of key materials such as iron ore, coal, bauxite, and manganese, the site at the confluence of the Subarnarekha and Kharkhai rivers was chosen as the site of the subcontinent's first iron and steel factory. By the year 1907, the factory began production and eastern India started its march towards industrialisation. This powerful narrative not only captured people's imagination but effectively made the region relevant to the nation almost entirely through the lens of industrial development alone. For most people, there was no significant history prior to the establishment of mines and factories with regard to this region. By extension, Adivasi people who lived in these parts prior to industrialisation were of little consequence as well.

It was in the late 1990s, when the state of Jharkhand was created primarily on a platform of greater political autonomy for the Adivasi populations of the region that another narrative of Adivasi culture and identity began to emerge. In addition to their dominance in the political realm, small but distinct signs of Adivasi arts, history and architecture gained prominence. A number of institutions were named after Birsa Munda, the Adivasi hero who fought against the colonial government and various non-Adivasi oppressors in defence of Adivasi rights to land and forests.[2] Statues of Birsa Munda and other rebel heroes began to be installed along highways at the entrance to villages and at various other locations within the landscape of Jharkhand. In the urban centres, examples of Adivasi visual and performing arts began to be used by industrial establishments as part of their corporate social responsibility initiatives. Jamshedpur now had a number of sites and events displaying Adivasi culture. Public fairs and sporting events began to be held on the birth anniversaries of important Adivasi figures and attracted large numbers of people from the villages and peripheries of the city. Adivasi song and dance routines featuring traditional musical instruments, elaborate costumes and headgear became part of the inauguration ceremonies of public events. Shops promoting Adivasi arts and crafts emerged. Decorative objects made of clay, metal and wood, and textiles with motifs of animals, plants or scenes of village life came to represent Adivasi culture. If one were to aggregate these various developments as constituting Adivasi heritage, a specific, simplistic imagination of this culture becomes evident. These events create an impression of Adivasis as people fond of simple song and dance, capable of great physical strength as demonstrated through sport, and intimately bound to land and forests as demonstrated through the materiality of their crafts. This in turn clearly distinguished Adivasis from the pushes and pulls of contemporary urban, industrial life (that characterises the rest of the region), and created the impression of a timeless, unchanged tradition. From a condition of near invisibility in previous decades, the Adivasi now emerged in popular imagination as a primitive figure, as the antithesis of industrial modernity.

Contrary to these stereotypes, however, academic scholarship has advanced a number of perspectives that recalibrate how Adivasi societies may be studied and understood. As early as the mid-twentieth century, Surajit Sinha challenged the idea of tribes as socially and ecologically isolated and internally homogenous communities. He compared two communities (Hill Marias in central India and Bhumij in eastern India) to argue that social and ecological isolation is not a universal feature of all Adivasi communities but varies across communities and regions. He discussed that the Hill Marias, though living in the hilly and jungle-clad regions of Bastar (in Madhya Pradesh), engaged in economic activities with other communities for essentials such as clothes and iron implements, had regular social interactions with other proximal communities through village markets and fairs, and shared a number of religious ritual similarities with local Hindu communities. Bhumij families, on the other hand, Sinha describes as landholding agriculturists who are much more closely connected to various Hindu communities they live and interact with.[3] Sinha's writing has an essentialising flavour, which is typical of ethnographic accounts of the time, but he clearly presents the Adivasis as a variegated demography. Recent studies on demography and local history add further nuance to this picture. Bandopadhyay analyses two important developments: demographic changes in the Chotanagpur region (what is modern-day Jharkhand) from the late eighteenth and through the early and mid-nineteenth centuries, and the establishment of colonial rule. Both these developments led to a period of Adivasi alienation from land and forest and conflicts between Adivasis and non-Adivasi outsiders.[4] Sen examines unusual archives such as Adivasi burial sites (which are marked by megalithic memorial stones and are used over subsequent generations) and village and land names to reveal a shifting landscape of Adivasi inhabitation.[5] He focuses on the Ho community and traces their historical movements, migration within Singhbhum, and finds that individual villages were successively occupied by different communities, each of which left their traces in the landscape. These narratives clearly suggest that the pre-industrial past of Singhbhum was not a forested idyll but a time of dynamic movements and conflict. The spread of industrialisation in the early twentieth century added new dimensions to the mix of Adivasi experience. The construction of railways and factories in this thickly forested landscape became possible through the employment of Adivasis as labourers. Notes left by early surveyors and engineers involved in the construction of the steel factory at Jamshedpur, for instance, mention Adivasi labourers, who lived in camps at the periphery of the construction sites.[6] Colonial land survey records make note of the substantial changes in demographic composition in Jamshedpur at the time of the establishment of the factory and in the wake of expansion in subsequent decades. While a paucity of records prevent the construction of a fuller picture, these archival hints leave no doubt that Adivasi communities were participant in, rather than isolated from the industrialisation and modernisation of the region. They allow the construction, to some extent at least, of adivasis as individual with some historical, economic, and political agency.[7]

Driving around Jamshedpur and the surrounding villages today, the complexities of history become evident in the patchwork of places and objects that constitute the contemporary landscape. At an obvious level, it comprises vast tracts of paddy fields, interspersed with reserved forests, i.e., clusters of trees or younger plantations that are managed by the State and mostly out of bounds for local villagers. Nestled within these are stone quarries or large and small factories. Strictly speaking, the forests, fields and factories belong to different agencies and to different orbits of economic logic, but they become interconnected in the everyday practices of the villagers. Fields are cultivated by villagers but owners of large tracts of land may employ poorer, non-landowning villagers as labourers. Similarly, stone quarries and brick kilns may be set up by villagers themselves or by people from outside, who then employ villagers. The State too employs villagers to build roads or dig tanks for water supply under State sponsored-employment guarantee schemes. Most villagers earn their subsistence from a combination of these modes of employment. They work in the paddy fields, supplement their daily needs by gathering firewood and other produce from the forests, and if the monsoon fails and agriculture suffers or if they do not own land, they work as wage labourers in the factories within the village and the region. The already variegated landscape of forests, fields and factories contains other sites and elements as well. Road building, electrification, solar street lights, water supply and institutions such as health clinics and village schools dot the landscape and carry signage describing the governmental or non-governmental agencies that provided them. Metal or cemented signage indicate both local and global organisations that provide such services to the villages. Provision of these kinds of infrastructure varies dramatically from village to village, but clearly register how these communities are connected to larger networks of economy and technology that potentially transform the everyday lives of the residents. Each such site or element embeds a story of how it came to be at that particular place. When considered as an accumulation over time, each Adivasi village appears as a dynamic site, shaped not only by the internal processes of the resident communities, but constantly negotiating economic, political and environmental forces outside of itself.

The potential of habitations to open windows into the past makes it an important archive for Adivasi histories, where the lack of documentary or material evidence is a well-recognised challenge. Much of what exists hinges on narratives of war or rebel heroes, or on ethnographic accounts from the early twentieth century. These narratives are important sources of information but are plagued by the biases of the historical moment that they were produced in. Many of these accounts were written during colonial times, when figures such as Birsa Munda presented challenges to colonial rule and are thus featured in particular ways in the records of the time. At the same time, in the early twentieth century, ethnographies of various Adivasi communities were in vogue, given the general rise of anthropology as a discipline and the interest in documenting the lives of various peoples of the subcontinent. These accounts record the life practices, belief systems, knowledge systems, and in some cases the built environments of various Adivasi communities in impressive detail but tend to have a broad essentialising tone. The lack of geographic or temporal specificities creates an impression of the characteristics of communities as being universal. As such, this limits the usability of ethnographic accounts as archives. Habitations, however, present an amalgam of past and present practices, memories and material engagements, and old structures and newer developments, all of which are shaped by the contingencies of time and place. By analysing how these habitations are produced, used and transformed, new dimensions of Adivasi history may be evoked.

The idea of habitations refers to both physical sites, i.e., the house, the village, the fields, and so on, and processes of Adivasi everyday life, i.e., domestic and community life, and the pursuit of basic needs, among other things. It also straddles past and present moments, and so the method of study requires some discussion. Throughout this book, I employ a combination of architectural analysis and ethnography of everyday life to develop the historical narrative. The ethnography reveals the negotiations and processes that shape the environment, and in a sense, identifies causal relationships between particular processes and the physical sites that emerge as a consequence. The architectural analysis of physical built forms on the other hand, reveals the trajectories of change. By triangulating contemporary sites and processes with the sites of the past, I extrapolate what everyday processes in the past may have been like. For instance, by observing and documenting the process of construction of a house, it becomes clear that clay, a common building material, is typically procured from people's own backyards or from places that may be considered equivalent of village commons. Simultaneously, the architectural analysis reveals that building materials gradually changed over time. Considering the network of materials being procured (rather than bought in exchange for cash) from the immediate surroundings of the village, I extrapolate that a shift in building materials may be linked to a shift in the surroundings of the village itself. I then attempt to account for these shifts in relation to the larger changes that took place in the region through the twentieth century. In this way, the minutiae of built forms and everyday life get connected to, and arguably recalibrate, meta-narratives such as colonisation, industrialisation and modernisation.

This project, or rather this approach, comes with two epistemological challenges. First, does the construction of narratives about the past, using experiences and processes from the present moment, assume the immutability of the communities in question? In other words, if contemporary practices are re-employed as a mode of reflecting upon and understanding Adivasis in the past, does this assume that Adivasi habitations have remained unchanged? Not necessarily, since both the built environment and the structures and processes of everyday life have clearly changed. Indeed, this is the starting point of this project itself. What remains constant, however, are some causal relationships as described above. These are shaped by the contingencies of time and place and may present a number of variations in terms of how and when they occur. In order to account for the variations, I draw from examples of different villages, each presenting a diversity of contexts of Adivasi habitations. If I take the example of building materials, or more specifically mud which is what houses are most commonly built with, the dominant mode of procurement is to dig up mud from the backyard of the house. When families do not have a sufficiently large backyard, or work as labourers and lack the labour required for digging, they may procure bricks for construction. Bricks, however, have to be paid for in cash, but given the dominantly agricultural economy of the villages, it is not common for villagers to have spare cash. It is therefore reasonable to conclude that the use of bricks indicates the lack of access to mud, or wealth in the form of spare cash. The chapters of this book explore multiple such processes across villages in order to identify a range of relationships in the production, use and transformation of Adivasi habitations. Rather than assuming that communities have not changed, the study focuses on patterns of change that illustrate how Adivasis have negotiated and inhabited their environment through the twentieth century.

The second challenge is linked to the question of interpretation. The focus on habitations inherently centres attention on the inhabitants, the Adivasi villagers. Rather than considering the villagers as simple representatives of their communities or of Adivasis as a collective, I draw out the specific negotiations of individuals in the course of their everyday lives. Herein lies both the potential and the problem. On the one hand, the characterisation of Adivasi habitations will require the collation of multiple individual experiences. Yet, the social and intellectual logic of individuals is not something that may be accessible to others, and more so to those such as myself who lie outside of their cultural realities. To illustrate, many Adivasi communities believe in spirits and witchcraft. In fact, most Adivasi communities believe that they co-habit this world together with spirits—clan spirits, family spirits and those of deceased ancestors. Different Adivasi religions are premised on the idea of propitiating the spirits in order to enjoy a peaceful life. They believe that spirits are both benevolent and malevolent and easily angered by transgressions which may be accidental in instances such as outsiders entering the sacred space of a family. Most communities also believe in witchcraft, and the potential of a woman bearing ill-will towards a family, or casting an evil eye on them. These beliefs have a definitive spatial dimension in that certain spaces of a dwelling are out of bounds for people who do not belong to the family. The transla-tion of this into practice varies considerably in both form and intensity across villages, but it nevertheless forms an important understructure to Adivasi notions of both dwelling and settlement. How are those who are outsiders to the beliefs that animate Adivasi life, to enter into their intellectual world, even if it is only in order to write about it? The approach I have taken is to focus on the logic of practice that these beliefs translate into. Without resorting to preconceived judgements or categories about why Adivasi villagers do certain things, the analysis unpacks *what* individuals do, against a backdrop of their possible motivations for doing so. So if the sacred space of an Adivasi house is closely enforced and guarded even though it does not often contain material belongings, this is clearly attributable to the belief in spirits residing in the dwelling. And when I am refused admission into such a space, while somebody else from the village is allowed to enter, it clearly highlights thresholds of familiarity based on degrees of spatial access. So throughout the study, while I may not personally believe in spirits or omens, it is, however, imperative to admit the possibility that somebody else's mode of being in the world may be premised on this belief.

Acknowledging the differences between the worlds of Adivasi villagers and my own conceptions and perceptions as an architect-researcher was central to reflecting on the ethnographic practices during fieldwork in the villages. Throughout this book, I share a number of fieldwork encounters in terms of how and where they took place and the conversations that ensued. These narratives supplement and indeed contextualise the analytical voice of the rest of the book. For instance, I mention how interior domestic spaces are out-of-bounds to outsiders, i.e., people who do not belong to the family, on account of sacredness and the belief in spirits. A description of this fact provides a nominal understanding of notions of dwelling. On the other hand, a description of an encounter where the villagers were palpably afraid of allowing me (as a woman and an outsider) into their sacred space for fear of bringing misfortune on the community powerfully evokes how the presence of spirits is woven into the practices of Adivasi everyday life. As villagers grew more familiar with me and were probably reassured that I do not bear any ill-will towards them or was unlikely to enter their houses without permission, they became less afraid, and in a few instances, I was invited into some rooms as well. The changes in people's reactions suggested that the belief in spirits and the closure of interior spaces is not absolute but is contingent upon the degree of interaction and familiarity with people outside the family and community. Discerning some of these realities was arguably only possible, and indeed plausible, when read in the context of my own presence and people's reactions towards me. By weaving my fieldwork encounters into architectural and anthropological analysis, and by moving between the intellectual frames of objective description and shared experience, I attempt to address the complexities of how one makes sense of Adivasi (or any other cultural group's) lives.

Of the many Adivasi communities in Jharkhand, this book focuses mostly on Santals, who are locally renowned for their domestic architecture. There are nearly 7.3 million Santals living primarily across the states of Jharkhand, West Bengal, Bihar, Odisha, but also spread in fewer numbers across other states and the neighbouring countries of Nepal and Bangladesh.[8] According to the 2011 Census of India, there are 2.75 million Santals in Jharkhand, constituting nearly thirty per cent of the total Adivasi population in the state.[9] Other numerically significant Adivasi communities in Jharkhand are Oraons, Hos and Mundas, while there are smaller populations of Kharwar, Lohra, Bhumij Kharia, and Birhor, to name just a few. More than 91 per cent of these Adivasi communities live in rural areas, typically in multi-community villages.[10] As a consequence, village communities are rarely neatly defined or internally homogenous groups. Rather, what one encounters is a range of distinctive and overlapping cultural, social and economic characteristics, within and outside different Adivasi communities. Languages, for instance, provide a good illustration of this complexity. Santals,

Hos, and Mundas speak their own languages, which belong to the Kherwar sub-group of the Austro-Asiatic family of languages. Consequently, there are a number of shared words and linguistic concepts between these groups, though the languages are distinct. What begins to lend further variation is that most Adivasi are bi- or even tri-lingual, being familiar with Hindi, Oriya, or Bengali depending on the part of south Jharkhand they live in. Over time, words from these languages have become incorporated into the everyday usage of Adivasi languages as well. For example, the house is known as *orak* (pronounced with the k nearly silent) by most communities, but they also occasionally use the word *ghor*, which is Bengali for house. While specifying the different rooms of the house, *orak* or *ghor* are pre-fixed with words describing the activity that takes place in that particular room. So the room for cooking may be known as *dakal orak* in Santali, where *dakal* refers to rice and so the term describes the room where rice is cooked. In regions where Bengali is the dominant language or widely spoken, the same space may be referred to as *ranna ghor,* where *ranna* is Bengali for cooking. While the absorption of terms across languages may appear self-evident in a multi-cultural demography, it hints at the complex intersections between the lives and cultures of Adivasi and non-Adivasi communities. The use of words from other languages for describing the most quotidian aspects of Adivasi life suggests the extent to which multi-cultural influences have coalesced into and form a part of Adivasi experiences.

The social life of different Adivasi communities is similarly complex. Early scholarship on Adivasis presented clear distinctive beliefs and practices as characteristic of these communities. For instance, it is well recognised that most Adivasi communities are divided into clans. Santal communities are divided into 12 clans, with each clan having specific mythical stories and a common last name, while Munda communities are typically divided into two clans, each tracing their origins to the priest and the headman of the village. In the area of village politics, many authors have documented that the governance of the village community across the different Adivasi societies hinges on the figure of the priest and the headman.[11] These two people are occasionally joined by a few other designated members who together constitute the village council. But these institutions, of both society and governance, are neither uniform nor stable. For instance, clans remain important identifiers but the lines are occasionally blurred with inter-community marriages, conversions to other religions, or gradual assimilation of Hindu religious practice. The clan at the level of families and individuals becomes a more multivalent construct than was previously imagined. Similarly, kinship bonds that are premised on participation in collective rituals are often disrupted or transformed on account of migration. Many Adivasi rituals take place in a sacred grove in the village and male members from all families of the village community are required to participate in the ritual event. When members of village families migrate, the norms of participation in village rituals also transform. In some cases, absent members may make a monetary contribution as a token of their participation, while in the more extreme cases, the rituals themselves may become decentralised and may take place at the level of the family instead of the community. Over time, this transforms the social bonds within the community. There are also other instances of individuals who transgress social norms. There are accounts of such individuals being excommunicated from the village. There are detailed ethnographic accounts of punishments meted out by Adivasi village councils and ritual ostracisation of villagers on offending other members of the community. The force of such practices today almost entirely depends upon the nature of authority that the village council exercises within a particular community on the one hand, and the status of the offending individuals on the other. It is not uncommon to find ostracised members continuing to live within the village community by converting to another religion and thus going outside the social purview of the village council, or being wealthy enough to be an important source of employment for other villagers, thus making it difficult for the council to apply any sanctions against them.

What further complicates community governance is the presence of different Adivasi groups in each village. In most cases, a village is led by a headman, who is traditionally descended from one of the families who first founded or settled the village. The lineage of the headman may consist of an uninterrupted chain of leaders of the village over generations, but may also get replaced by a more popular or competent individual, or face competition from members of other communities residing in the village. In some instances, the traditional headman may be reduced to a ritual figurehead while the actual negotiations and management of the village may be carried out by other individuals or groups such as members of the state administration. What this illustrates is that traditional Adivasi social and political institutions form a rather loose understructure for contemporary village societies, and range from exercising considerable authority to being nominal entities invoked on special occasions alone.

When discussing the overlaps between different Adivasi groups, it is crucial to address the similarities and differences between Adivasis and other non-Adivasi communities such as Mahatos and Gops, who also live in significant numbers across the Singhbhum region. Beteille presents compelling analysis to suggest that the Adivasis or tribes are too 'amorphous' and 'assorted' to be distinguished as a particular type of society.[12] He makes his case by starting with the historical origins of Adivasi identity formation, where he suggests that conceptions of tribe were neither clearly formulated nor systematically applied and the label included a wide range of small and large social formations, characterised by varied social structures and economic practices ranging from forest subsistence to large-scale agriculture. Contemporary Adivasi and non-Adivasi rural societies continue to share a number of similarities, while also perpetuating and emphasising [their] collective identities in remarkably similar ways. In fact, Beteille suggests that the tribe/non-tribe or Adivasi/non-Adivasi distinction is made by anthropologists rather than by economists or historians.[13] The shift in identity-politics is reflected in the currency of terms like 'tribe' and 'Adivasi'. The term Adivasi is a generic one and typically refers to (descendants of) original inhabitants. It is often used synonymously with 'tribe' but implies, what Rycroft and Dasgupta refer to as a 'range of historically defined, contested and mediated indigeneities'.[14] In comparison, 'tribe' presumes a primitive, 'isolated, self-contained and socially homogenous' social formation, and is inherently more static in the conception of the group it refers to.[15] While this may appear as a rather long view of a context that I have thus far dealt with and described in terms of grounded details, this broad ambiguity translated into very specific identifiers in the field. When interacting with different villagers, I found complex and contextually varying usages of the terms 'tribe' and 'Adivasi'. Nowadays, most Santal villagers used the English word 'tribe' or the

Hindi term 'Adivasi' to describe themselves. This is clearly drawn from narratives used by the State or by political regimes where these two terms are used respectively. What made the descriptions more complex were the people described as others. In some cases, Santal villagers described themselves as Adivasis and their Hindu and Muslim neighbours as 'others', while in some cases even other Adivasi groups such as Mundas were described as 'others'. The terms of reference typically depended on the context of the conversation, which demonstrates that the manner in which communities identify themselves depends upon the particular contexts of interaction. It is this ambiguity, or rather multivalence, that Beteille refers to when he argues that the larger structures of Adivasi norms and identity are drawn from external sources, of both contemporary and historical vintage.

The issue of identity becomes important since this book focuses primarily on Santals while recognising that they are linked in complex ways to other communities in the region and beyond. So the habitations that I analyse in the following chapters are not unique to Santal communities. At the same time, they are not entirely generic either. As I mentioned earlier, when introducing Santals, they are locally renowned for producing precisely constructed and beautifully painted and decorated mud houses. As the colonial scholar W.G. Archer noted, 'of all the other tribes of eastern India, none has quite the same relish for neatly ordered houses, the same capacity for tidy spacious living or the same genius for domestic architecture.'[16] The craftsmanship and visual appeal is interesting considering that nearly all rural communities build their houses using the same materials and nearly the same technologies. Further, the configurations of space within the houses are also quite similar. It takes further probing into the use, taboos and nomenclature of spaces to reveal subtle differences between the houses and dwelling practices of communities. Additionally, there are different levels of similarity and difference. For instance, houses within a village are likely to share greater similarities in terms of spatial configuration and distribution of activities, even if the families belong to different communities. At the same time, Santal houses in different regions share some broad architectural characteristics such as the precision of construction described earlier. Each house, therefore, emerges in the interplay of local social and material conditions on the one hand and some aspects of what may be called a collective cultural memory of the group on the other. Methodologically speaking, what follows is not a study of Santals as a cultural or architectural whole, but as a collation of multiple individuals, sites and processes. Each of these is investigated in terms of their specific trajectories of productive and transformative influences, and together, constitute a narrative about Santal habitations. The multivalent characterisation provides enough threads to evoke a sense of Adivasi experiences in the past and present moments. The narrative is not about houses alone, but of Adivasi history as a collation of diverse engagements that are in part defined by habitations.

Chapter 1

The *Orak* and Its History

I first visited a Santal village in the blistering heat of May in the year 2001. I was searching for a research topic for the final semester of my undergraduate architecture degree. Accompanying me was Fusari Chacha, an elderly gentleman who was deeply involved in various social projects in the rural areas to the south of Jamshedpur and was familiar with most villages in the vicinity. After discussing briefly about how we would travel to the villages, it was decided that cycling would be the best alternative. Two cycles and two bottles of water wrapped in gunny were procured and we set off. We turned off the highway into a dust road. We cycled past dry fields covered with rough stubs left over from the previous year's harvest, clusters of trees with the ground below them covered with dry leaves, and an occasional villager on a cycle carrying various kinds of loads. The road was full of stones and quite bumpy, a fact accentuated by our travel on cycles. We rode on for quite some time before we arrived at a village.

It was rather quiet and not a person was in sight. This was understandable given the heat in the middle of the day. The village had a few mud houses built at some distance from each other on either side of what was mostly a mud track. There was a hand pump by the side of the road, and a pig tethered by a long rope under a tree. This is where the village precinct began, Fusari Chacha said. We paused for a drink of water from our bottles and Fusari Chacha went looking for someone to speak to. We met a group of women sitting under a tree. They were a self-help group and had gathered for a weekly meeting. Fusari Chacha introduced me as someone who wanted to know something about rural houses. The women were amused. These were poor people's mud houses. Didn't the city have better houses? Still, we chatted briefly about how they built their mud houses using local materials. We also chatted about the villagers waiting for the rains to grow paddy, and the importance of women making small savings to sustain their families during the lean periods. Like most city-dwellers, I vaguely knew about some of these things, but the intimacy and materiality of rural life was new to me. As I absorbed the sites and information, we decided to move onto the next village. An hour later, we arrived at the second village. Here, Fusari Chacha knew someone, so we went straight to their house. The house had two rooms also made of mud and the walls were covered with some slogans about a government sanitation campaign. We went in through the door and entered a courtyard. We sat on a seat built against the base of the wall as the family gathered to chat with us. The conversation moved from the shortage of water in the middle of summer, to how some of the poorer families in the village barely had enough rice to feed themselves. How did they survive, I asked. They told me that people took odd jobs around the village such as grazing other people's cows and working on neighbouring quarries, and those who were able, made the trip to Ghatsila or Jamshedpur to find work. Agriculture was simply not enough. After this sobering conversation, we decided to move on. It was nearly lunchtime and the heat was peaking. We decided to take a break and then resume travelling later in the afternoon.

The economic realities and movement of the villagers made an overwhelming impression on me after the morning visit, but the first, albeit blurry, patterns of the built environment also began to surface as I ate my lunch at a *dhaba*, roadside eateries found on long highways. Most of the houses we saw were constructed entirely of mud and were roofed with wooden beams and rafters covered with thatch or clay tiles. Fusari Chacha mentioned that the houses were quite old, ranging from 10 to 50 years and occasionally even older. So contrary to what one may imagine, mud construction clearly survived the heavy summer showers and monsoon rains that the region typically received. Most villages appeared to have one central street and the houses were built on either side and at varying distances. Some villages had houses right next to each other while in others they were built further apart. Each house had some kind of yard, distinguishable from the rest of the area as a cleared and plastered patch of ground. The landscape was dotted with trees, but except for small patches of wilderness, there were no large tracts of dense forest. Instead, we saw row upon row of eucalyptus or other trees, often within fenced enclosures with a sign identifying the state forestry department as the owner of these plantations. Nearly five months had passed since the previous harvest of paddy and the next cycle of agricultural work would now begin only after July, when the monsoon rains had irrigated the fields. So most villagers were away seeking work at other places. It was people from such villages, who could be seen employed in stone quarries along the highway, selling vegetables in markets across the region, or seeking work outside the factories in Jamshedpur. The highway was an important spine connecting the villages to these other sites. Places such as the *dhaba* I was lunching in, became important nodes. Around me sat a few workers from nearby construction sites, a few truck drivers and other travellers, and the place was clearly a meeting point.

After a nap to beat the afternoon heat, we set off again and arrived at a village called Herang. The difference from the villages I had visited earlier was immediately apparent. Herang had a markedly different architectural appeal as the walls of the houses were painted in red, ochre, blue and black bands. The houses were made of mud, just like the houses we saw in the morning, but the walls were meticulously smooth and had a particularly neat appearance. Rows of houses lined either side of the street, which itself was spotlessly clean. Since it was later in the afternoon, there were a few people in the street, many of them tying cows, which had returned from grazing, to pegs lined along the front walls of the houses. We visited one elderly man that Fusari Chacha knew, and I took the opportunity to take a closer look at these remarkable houses. We entered a central yard around which lay the rooms of the house. They explained that there was one room for cooking and eating, one for storing things, and they tied their cows under a shed which lay on one side of the yard. The courtyard was also very clean and the floor was plastered with what appeared to be cow dung. I expressed surprise at the meticulousness of the house and Fusari Chacha explained that this was a Santal village. The villages that I visited in the morning were those of Munda and Mahato families. It was locally known, Fusari Chacha said, that no one built houses with as much precision or decorated the walls with as much colour and flair as Santals (Figures 1.1 and 1.2).

The visit to Herang, was for me, the beginning of nearly two decades of documentation of Santal houses. I travelled across the

Figure 1.1 *View of Santal Village Street*

Figure 1.2 *Santal Houses in Herang*

Singhbhum region and in nearly every instance, I found that Santal houses were crafted and decorated in ways that visually distinguished them from those of other communities. What emerged over time, however, was that Santal houses were similar in many ways to those of other Adivasi and non-Adivasi communities in some villages, and yet, were different in other places. Domestic architectural traditions, rather than being singular along lines of Adivasi ethnicity, are a rather variegated landscape of house layouts, construction technology and decorative practices. Building materials across the Singhbhum region (and even beyond, extending all the way to north Jharkhand) were largely the same and yet, mud or stone is used in slightly different ways in different regions, resulting in subtle differences in the physical structure of the house. Internally, houses often had largely similar configurations and yet the allocation of activities varied in accordance with specific cultural practices or livelihoods. Domestic architecture could not be delineated into neat categories along lines of either community or locality. It presented instead multiple points of archi-tectural convergence and divergence. In order to navigate this complex meshwork of social, ecological, and historical forces, in the interplay of which Santal and other Adivasi habitations were located, it made methodological sense to begin enquiry with one site, i.e., the house, and more specifically the Santal house. Later, when I discuss the various aspects of Santal houses, I discuss points of correspondence and differ-ences with other communities, regions, and time periods, as the case may be.

ENTERING THE *ORAK*

One of the smaller Santal houses I visited belonged to a widow in the Banhatu village (Figure 1.3).[17] She lived with her only daughter in one room which was built almost directly on the *kulhi*, which is the central street of the village. The front walls of Santal houses are nearly always blank, with no openings except for the front door. Santals and other Adivasis in the region have a strong belief in witchcraft and there is a palpable fear of outsiders casting an evil eye and brining misfortune upon the family. One of the protections against this is the physical structure of the house itself: the blank walls protect the interior space

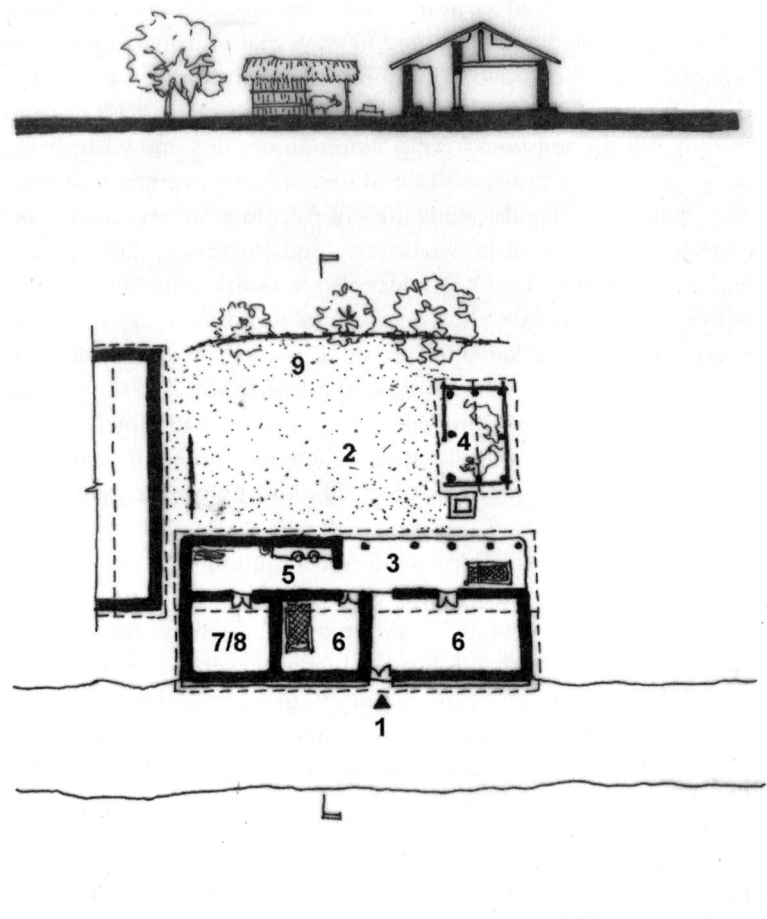

0 1 2   5   10M

Figure 1.3 *Widow's Small House in Phulgoda*

The distribution of activities is as follows: 1, entrance; 2, *racha*; 3, *chali* (verandah); 4, animal shelter; 5, cooking area; 6, sleeping area; 7, *bhitar*; 8, grain store; 9, *barge* (backyard garden)

Figure 1.4 *View of Blank Wall along the Street*

of the house from being exposed to an outsider's gaze (Figure 1.4). As we walk in through the front door, we enter a vestibule-like space which leads into a yard, known as *racha*. The room on one side of the vestibule (and the vestibule itself) were recently added and are used by the daughter and her husband, while the older room on the other side is kept locked. The widow adamantly refused to let us enter or even tell us anything about the interior, and so it followed that this must be the *bhitar*, which is a sacred space and the most private part of Santal houses. Santals believe that they co-habit the earth with various spirits, including those of deceased ancestors. Within the house, the *bhitar* is the abode of spirits, and people, apart from members of the family, are not permitted to enter for the fear of displeasing the spirits. Outside the *bhitar* was a partially covered shed which had a mud stove built into a corner, which was clearly used as a kitchen. The *racha* had a shed on one side, which was used to shelter cattle at night. Below the eaves in the newly added room was another mud stove, which was used by the daughter and her husband for cooking their meals. A mud stove in the middle of the *racha* appeared unused, but the widow mentioned that it was used for parboiling paddy. At the back, the *racha* was fenced using a panel made of branches and wooden strips tied together and the *barge* or backyard lay beyond the fence. Apart from the fence, the *barge* was distinguishable from the *racha* on account of the ground surface. The floor of the *racha* was smoothly plastered with mud and cow dung, while the *barge* was left as it is, i.e., covered in grass, stubble and mud. Beyond the *barge* lay clusters of trees, and further, the paddy fields cultivated by the villagers.

A more typical mid-size house belongs to Neelkanth Hansdah in Bhagabondi (Figure 1.5). He lives with his wife, two children, widowed mother and unmarried sister. Also built directly on the *kulhi*, we enter through a verandah which opens into the *racha*. The *racha* in this case is enclosed with rooms on all sides. The verandah at the entrance is where the family meets visitors. Neelkanth Hansdah is a village official and has a number of visitors throughout the day. This was also where I spent most of my time conversing with the family and other neighbours during my field visits. Additionally, there are separate rooms for sleeping—one for Hansdah, his wife and children, and one used by his sister and mother. These areas are also used to store the family's annual stock of paddy. The house has two separate areas for cooking—one larger fully-enclosed kitchen used by Hansdah's wife, and a stove under the eaves in one corner of the *racha* used by his mother. One room is used to shelter cows, while a second shelter was added to the back of the house as their herd grew. The *bhitar* was not separate but a segregated corner within the sleeping room used by Neelkanth Hansdah and his wife. As the eldest male member of the family, he offered worship in the *bhitar*. His unmarried sister, however, prayed at a shrine she had set up in a different room. As such, Santal women do not routinely participate in family rituals conducted by the men, and instead light an oil lamp or an incense stick in front of a mud platform or the sacred *tulsi* plant in the *racha*. Many Santals include Hindu deities such as Shiva and Kali in their ritual practices, which is what Hansdah's sister does as well. The difference in deity and rituals is registered through a different space for her prayers as well. From the *racha*, a vestibule leads towards the back of the house into the *barge*, where the family stores agricultural equipment, bales of straw, and on one side, grows vegetables for their own consumption. They also have a place for washing utensils, with the water draining away towards the vegetable patch for reuse.

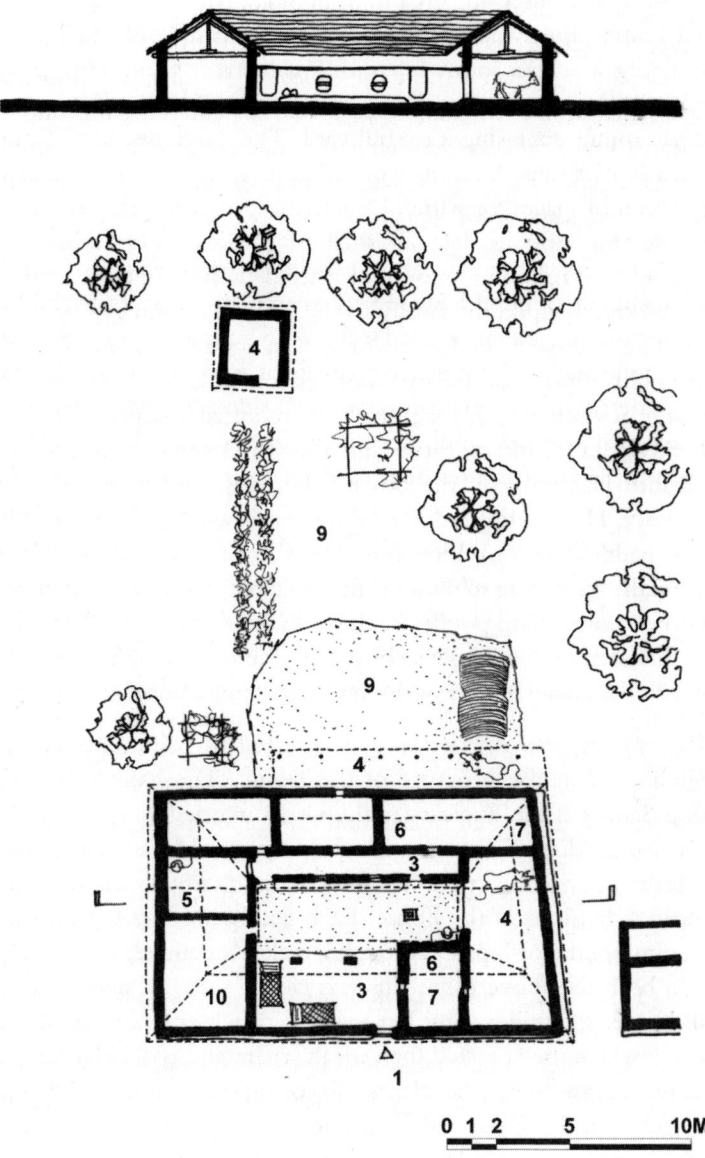

Figure 1.5 *Mid-size House in Bhagabondi*

The distribution of activities is as follows: 1, entrance; 2, *racha*; 3, *chali* (verandah); 4, animal shelter; 5, cooking area; 6, sleeping area; 7, *bhitar*; 8, grain store; 9, *barge* (backyard garden); 10, shrine of another deity

These two houses are broadly representative of the spectrum of Santal houses, the widow's house being an example of small houses comprising a single room separating the street from a yard, and Neelkanth Hansdah's house being an example of a larger house with multiple rooms enclosing a central yard. The difference in size apart, the two houses share a number of similarities in terms of the internal designation of spaces for particular activities. In both cases, rooms are designated for cooking, sleeping, sheltering animals, and storing grain. The number of rooms or amount of space dedicated for these activities depends directly upon the family's need and the resources available to them. The widow owned a small patch of agricultural land but only started cultivation with the arrival of her son-in-law.[18] Consequently, their annual stock of paddy was small and required less space. They also had only four heads of cattle and one shed sufficed as a shelter. Neelkanth Hansdah, on the other hand, was a relatively wealthier landowner. He employed a few labourers to work his fields and had surplus paddy, part of which was stored in his house for consumption and the remaining sold for profit. He also had a larger herd of cows and other animals and poultry such as chickens and pigs, all of which were sheltered in their large backyard. Agricultural wealth usually correlates to the elaborateness of the internal configuration of the *orak*.

Rooms are also divided and designated for different activities depending upon the structure of the family. The basic family unit among Santals is the nuclear family, i.e., a married couple and their unmarried children. When sons in a family grow older and get married, they form a new family unit. These units are clearly distinguishable in the spatial divisions of the house. Each family unit has separate areas for cooking and worship, and though less clearly defined, also for sleeping. In both the above cases, this was clearly seen. In spite of a very small house, the widow and her married daughter had two different stoves in which they cooked their meals separately, as did Hansdah and his sister and mother. The places of worship were similarly divided. The widow had a *bhitar* and a separate shrine where her son-in-law offered worship to other deities, and Hansdah and his sister had separate places for worship as well. The cooking and sleeping areas are separated along family lines in nearly all circumstances, but the division of the *bhitar* tends to be more varied. There are instances where every family

Figure 1.6 *View of Racha*

unit does not have a separate *bhitar* or shrine and only the eldest married male member of the family is designated with a *bhitar* and other men join in the ritual activities. Based on such spatial divisions, it is evident that elderly couples, unmarried siblings, or a widowed parent all become distinctive family units. They may live in the same house but cook and pray separately.

The *racha* is not spatially divided between family units as much as the other parts of the house are (Figure 1.6). Different units, however, do have distinctive markers of their use of the yard. The *tulsi pinda* or mud platforms used for worship are one such marker. Bhagabondi, which had a number of extended families living in one house, had a few instances where two *pinda* were built within a *racha*. Their separate ownership was further underscored by gestures such as a small fence, separating the sacred space of one *pinda* from the other. Mud stoves built in the *racha* are also used by specific family members. These are not usually used for daily cooking but for parboiling paddy prior to husking. Large pots are piled with paddy and water, and the grain is left to soak and steam in the hot water before it is dried and husked. Separate mud stoves are found, particularly in houses where two or three married brothers lived together. Since each of them cultivates land separately, the harvesting and processing of paddy was also done separately, leading to the demarcation of mud stoves and threshing stones within the *racha*. At first glance, the *racha* appears less clearly divided as compared to the rooms of the house, but patterns of use slowly reveal that different family units notionally lay claim to different parts of the yard. In a few instances, this claim was made explicit through the painting of the walls. One house with three family units—an elderly couple, unmarried daughters, and a widowed daughter-in-law and her child—had the walls of the *racha* painted differently. It looked initially like a simple pattern but operated in conjunction with the stoves and *pinda* to create specific territories that each unit regularly occupied.

By juxtaposing inter-generational changes in family structure—particularly through marriage and on account of inheritance—to the layout, it appears that the house is nearly constantly in flux. The most obvious change is from one generation to another, when sons get married and the spaces within the house get subdivided to accommodate this new family unit or they build a separate house next to their parents' house. On a smaller scale, changing needs lead to small additions. Neelkanth Hansdah added a shed for additional cattle, temporarily building it with wood and some branches to create an enclosure. His plan is to build this in mud and turn it into a more permanent part of the house. Right next door, Hansdah's widowed sister-in-law decided to add a small shop to her one-room house since she had no other source of livelihood. She added a room to one side and opened it up to the street to serve as a shop window. The break in the annual agricultural cycle, which lasts between January and May, is the time when most families take up construction activities. It is at this time that the house undergoes varying degrees of transformation. The materiality of the house, i.e., the fact that mud and wooden members can be reused is an important factor that aids rebuilding. Most significantly, this explained why the Santal houses I encountered were of such varying forms and configurations. The house is not an artefact, physically frozen once built, but more akin to a process with constant addition, division, and adaptation. So when Fusari Chacha and the villagers described the houses as being quite old, they were not referring to the structure of the house per se, but to the fact that many of these sites have been inhabited over generations.

One important factor that affects the form of the houses is the availability of land, particularly in cases of the division of the house after the marriage of a son. In villages such as Haudah, where houses were built at considerable distances from each other, a newly married son and his wife built a new house right next to the older one. The new house was also built along the *kulhi* with its own set of rooms and yards and would develop over time in the manner described earlier. Over two or three generations of such building, the land owned by a family fragments to such an extent that it is no longer possible for new houses to be built. The *kulhi* is densely built up with houses right next to each other, as is seen in Bandhudih and Bhagabondhi today. It is at this point that houses are internally divided to accommodate new family units. In some villages today, the density is such that three or four family units live in the same house, each internally dividing their territories.

The variations in size notwithstanding, some key relationships define the internal configuration of the house and remain more or less constant through various transformations. The entrance of the house from the *kulhi* is always a threshold marking the separation of domestic spaces from the relatively public space of the *kulhi*. Considering that the *kulhi* is a site of gathering and casual conversation in addition to being the spine of movement within the village, it is a significant social institution. As such, all houses are built with direct access to the *kulhi*. So it also becomes important to position the front door and blank front walls as barriers protecting the interiors from public gaze. Internally, rooms are designated for cooking, sleeping, sheltering animals, storing grain and as the *bhitar*. These are, without exception among rural Santal communities at least, the spatial and functional constituents of domestic space. The *racha* is nearly always the locus of the family's activities. At first glance, nothing specific appears to happen here but this is where, every day, the women spend their time doing household chores, children play, men and elderly people sit around and talk. The *racha* is in direct contrast with the rooms since it is a site of much activity compared to the rooms which may almost be considered as places of storage, be it grain or cattle. The more a family's wealth, the larger the number of rooms, but the family continues to conduct much of its socialising and household chores within the *racha*.

THE *ATH-CHALA* AND OTHER HISTORICAL POSSIBILITIES

Throughout my fieldwork in the villages, I had been asking how houses were built in the past. There is little historical evidence and so this was a rather open-ended question. As it became evident that the houses had undergone significant transformation over time, the question began to seem even more pertinent.

It was clear that the houses developed from single-roomed structures to larger *orak* with yards in the centres. This change was linked to resources and family size and was not really evolutionary in a way that one may consider the single-room-type *orak* as the temporal predecessor of the ones with the yard. Villagers' own descriptions tended to be vague. In most cases, villagers mentioned that the present-day houses were already quite old, built usually by the previous or even earlier generations. The most common answer was '*aisa hi tha*' meaning it was just like this. A breakthrough of sorts came when I was shown a house in the village of Bandudih that the villagers knew to be much older than the other houses in the village.

The house belonged to a Munda family, and I was shown around by Moni Singh, the wife of the owner (Figure 1.7). It formed part of a cluster of Munda houses which on the outside looked exactly like an *orak*. We entered through the front door into the *racha,* which had rooms on all sides. One of the rooms, however, was different. It was a higher volume with a gable roof. Internally, it was made up of two parts—an inner room with a long room, known as chali, encircling it on all sides. The inner room was high enough to accommodate a loft, which was accessed from the verandah. The lower space was used for storing grain, while the loft was used for storing other household items. Two sides of the verandah were used for sheltering cattle, while the space right at the entrance had a *dhenki* (oil press). The layout was distinctly different from that of the *orak* and it was known as an *ath-chala*. *Ath* means eight and *chala* refers to the sloping sides of the roof (Figure 1.8). Had it not been explicitly pointed out as an older house, it would have escaped my notice altogether. In fact, in many instances, I did document houses with concentric layouts but considering that they usually formed one of the rooms around the yard of an *orak*,

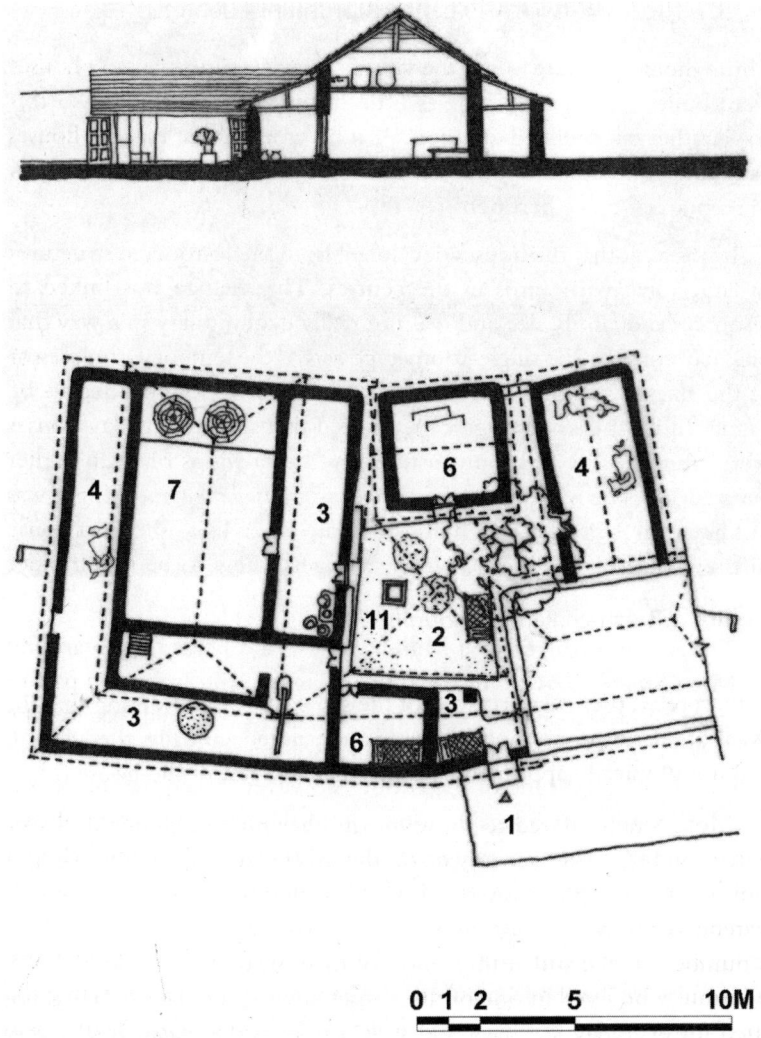

Figure 1.7 Ath-chala *House with Additional Rooms Added Later*

The distribution of activities is as follows: 1, entrance; 2, *racha*; 3, *chali* (verandah); 4, animal shelter; 5, cooking area; 6, sleeping area; 7, *bhitar*; 8, grain store; 9, *barge* (backyard garden); 11, *tulsi* (sacred plant)

Figure 1.8 Ath-chala *in Bandudih Village*

I interpreted them as variations of the same type. Considering that the walls of the house are mud-plastered and painted annually, the *ath-chala* did not physically appear to be older than the rest of the house.

Moni Singh offered to show me another house like this. I readily agreed and we made our way down the street towards a cluster of Santal houses. Like in the previous case, this cluster too belonged to an extended family, and had emerged over two generations. There were a number of *orak* and at the centre of these stood the *ath-chala*. Anjali Murmu, who lived in one of the houses said that the *ath-chala* was not used for everyday activities and served only as the *bhitar*. It was very old, though she could not put a figure to the age of the structure. She guessed that it was built by her husband's uncle or a similar relative before she got married. As we walked around the house, I could see that it too had a concentric layout—a central space and a verandah on three sides. The inner space was used as a *bhitar,* and as in most cases, Anjali Murmu was reluctant to let me look inside the room. We walked around the verandah and she pointed to a mud stove, indicating the place formerly used for cooking, and to some stumps in the ground, indicating the place for sheltering cattle. Unlike Moni Singh's house, this *ath-chala* was not in use except for ritual activities. We returned to the question of age. Both Moni Singh and Anjali Murmu stated that such houses were no longer built. They had only ever encountered these examples built by previous generations of their family.

The *ath-chala* is distinctly different from the more common *orak* in terms of layout. Where the *orak* schematically developed from a single-roomed structure into an aggregation of rooms enclosing a yard, the *ath-chala* was already internally differentiated to accommodate different activities of the house. Moreover, the *bhitar* was distinctly located within the inner space of the concentric layout. This discovery led to two propositions. First, on the basis of the different layouts in the various houses I had documented so far, I could identify parts which were clearly of the *ath-chala* type and could therefore be identified as an older core to which other rooms had been added over time. What this meant was that some present-day *orak* had their origins not in a single room, as I had outlined in the previous pattern, but in an *ath-chala*. This accounted for the variations in layouts that I had observed, and which had appeared confusing at first glance. Some *orak* developed from single rooms while other developed from an *ath-chala*. So rather than being different kinds of houses, the variations emerged on account of its genesis and development. The second point was that there were no recently built *ath-chala* houses. In recent memory, the typical layout of the house was nearly always the *orak* beside or around a *racha*. It seemed possible that the *ath-chala,* at some point in the past, gave way to the *orak* as the common layout for houses. This raised further questions of the period over which this shift may have occurred and whether there was any evolutionary link between the *ath-chala* and the present-day houses.

Before addressing these questions, it is worth reflecting on why it was so difficult to identify the *ath-chala* as an older type of house when it is so physically distinctive, and commonly known to the villagers as an older type of house. As I mentioned earlier, most *ath-chala* formed part of present-day *orak*. Considering that all houses are built and transformed over time, the *ath-chala* was part of that continuum of dwelling transformation for the families who inhabited it. From the lens of analysis, it was a different layout type, but for the inhabitants, it was one of the many stages of transformation that the house had undergone. So when I asked about older houses, it is likely that the villagers did not really distinguish the *ath-chala* as an older type in comparison to the *orak,* and hence, responded by saying that their houses had always been like this. This also flagged the notion that architectural transformation was not a watershed moment but a gradual change possibly over a considerable period of time.

Returning to the question of the period when this transformation may have occurred, one clue came from the distribution of the *ath-chala* type houses across the region of Singhbhum. Among the villages where I carried out fieldwork, Bandudih and Haudah have examples of *ath-chala* houses while Bhagabondi does not. On the basis of colonial maps and land records of the Singhbhum region, I knew that the former were older villages as compared to Bhagabondi. For instance, the earliest known colonial map was produced between 1859 and 1863 and includes the names of Bandudih, Ramgarh and Haudah.[19] These villages must have been reasonably well-established settlements since they find mention in the maps. Bhagabondi which does not feature on this map, may have been non-existent or a very small hamlet, too insignificant to find mention in a survey. According to Neelkanth Hansdah, who is one of the educated villagers and often helps others with property papers and other interactions with district officials, Bhagabondi first found official mention somewhere in the early 1900s. Seeing that there are no *ath-chala* houses in Bhagabondi and nobody recollects there ever having been one, it is plausible that by this time the *orak* type houses were already being built. Somewhere, over the five decades, from the mid-nineteenth to the early twentieth century, the *ath-chala* probably went out of currency. While this may seem like a tenuous conjecture, the pattern plays out in other villages as well. Ramgarh, Herang, Phulgoda, Pipdih, to name just a few, have examples of *ath-chala* houses. In each case, the villagers attest that these are the oldest houses in the village and they are all mentioned in the mid-nineteenth-century map. Newer villages such as Chota Bondudih, Taloidih, Lelang do not have a single *ath-chala* house and instead have large *orak*, which develop to such sizes over time.

The question of an evolutionary link remains. Did the *ath-chala* transform into the *orak* or replace it? The latter is more plausible given that the logic of growth of the two layout types is very different. The *orak* is a clearly incremental type of layout, which begins with a single volume and the subsequent rooms get added perpendicularly to enclose the *racha*. The *ath-chala* on the other hand appears to be a more fully formed layout with the two concentric spaces being built at the same time rather than appearing incrementally. This is particularly supported by the technicalities of constructing the mud walls and adding the wooden roof (which is discussed in detail in the next chapter). The inner room is higher than the outer verandah. The wooden beams of the verandah roof are fixed within the inner walls, ruling out any possibility of later additions. The differences in the process of growth suggests that the *ath-chala* and the *orak* clearly belong to two separate trajectories of domestic architecture.

In terms of the spatial distribution of domestic activities, the *ath-chala* is very similar to a mid-sized *orak*. In both cases, there are discrete rooms or clearly defined spaces for cooking, sleeping, storing grain, sheltering animals, and the *bhitar*. Such activities, especially the storage of paddy and keeping animals are typical of families whose primary source of livelihood is agriculture. Families that are primarily made up of wage earners, for instance, tend to buy grains periodically rather than storing an annual supply, and keep smaller animals such as chickens rather than cattle. Based on this, the *ath-chala* was clearly a house type inhabited by cultivator families. Prof. Digambar Hansdah recollects similar attributes about his own childhood home, which was an *ath-chala*.[20] His father was a landowner and he recalls the presence of a *dhenki* (oil press) right in front of the main door of the house. Seeds were pressed to extract oil for consumption by the family. The family also stored paddy in large baskets woven out of straw. The *racha* in this case was a yard in front of the house and had a large dovecot-like shed, where a number of pots were hung from the roof for pigeons to nest in. Putting this anecdotal evidence together, a picture emerges of the *ath-chala* as a house built by families already involved in agriculture in the early twentieth century.

Alongside these discussions, conversations were also pointing towards a different, smaller and almost shack-like house that was built in the past. Elderly villagers remembered houses that were like a *jhupdi,* meaning shack. They described it as being built using wood and leaves, located within forests, and that it could be built quickly. Families in those days did not stay in one location permanently. As they moved from one location to the other, the house was built anew. Since they remembered seeing these shacks in their childhood, one can assume that they were in use in the mid-twentieth century. Before moving ahead, it is important to flag here my dependence on conversations and memories for eliciting information about the past. As such, I was asking a simple question, viz., what were houses like, in the past. What made the answer complicated was, first, the sense of time and what the 'past' referred to. Most villagers did not think about the past in calendric time, as most of us do. Their references were often generational, and so they remembered temporal milestones such as the age of the house in relation to the member of the previous generation who had built it. So an old house could have been built by a man's grandfather, but that may refer to a time anywhere between 20 or 50 years ago. Second, given that houses grow and transform over time, and families occasionally move from one place of inhabitation to another, it is nearly impossible to pin down the time in which a particular house may have been built. The place of dwelling is in near constant transition, at least across generations, if not over shorter periods of time, and most houses are amalgams of buildings from various periods. Finally, there is the challenge of how rural Adivasi societies remember the past. There is a mythic past memorialised through ritual practices and oral traditions. Villagers also have some cognition of the important events in national history. One villager, for instance, referred to the year of her marriage as the year when a 'woman prime minister' was assassinated.[21] Houses, however, are located within the mundane sphere of the everyday and do not particularly merit a distinctive place in people's memory. Consequently, my method was broadly recursive. I used small cues, such as being shown the oldest house in Bandudih, to develop a proposition, which when discussed with other villagers and scholars, led to a consolidation or further development of the idea. So, the villagers' vague memories of a shack-like structure provided the cue, and the subsequent conversation with Professor Hansdah provided the name *kumbha*, which allowed more focused future enquiry.

I had not come across any *kumbha* in the villages that I visited. All the houses without exception were built using mud. The only thing that indicated what a *kumbha* may have been like was the temporary sheds and enclosures that were made by families as a first step towards extending part of the house. These extensions were made of branches tied together to wood or bamboo strips to create a flat panel, which was known as *jhanti*. These were used to create walls, roofs or fences depending on the need. The ease and speed of making a *jhanti* appeared to match the villagers' description of the *kumbha*. When I asked about it, they concurred that the walls of the *kumbha* were made of *jhanti* and the roof was thatched with leaves. I finally chanced upon a *kumbha* when visiting a Birhor community in the village of Belpahadi (Figure 1.9). Here, and more generally, the Birhor families were primarily sustaining themselves by trapping small animals and gathering produce from neighbouring forests. They did not own land and were not involved in agriculture even as labourers. Belonging to the poorest strata of village society, the state had provided a concrete frame and a few brick walls to the Birhor families for building houses. Not having any additional resources, however, the families had built the wooden

Figure 1.9 Kumbha *Built by a Birhor Family*

kumbha within the concrete frame. The walls were similar to the Santal *jhanti,* and the roof was thatched with layers of dried leaves. The *kumbha* comprised a single room on one end of which was a stove. At the other end, the family's belongings were stored. If this can be considered as a model for the Santal *kumbha,* this corner would have also been the *bhitar.* From a mere memory, an image of the *kumbha* was beginning to take form.

The temporariness of the *kumbha* is related to the fact that Birhor families are not landowners or significantly involved in agriculture. Both the *ath-chala* and the present-day *orak* have agriculture-related activities and spaces as an important characteristic. They both have spaces for storing grains and sheltering animals, which are associated directly with architecture. The yards have mud stoves, an important element, albeit one which is periodically used. The size of the yard, in terms of the patch of ground which is plastered with mud, is itself directly linked to the space required to dry and thresh the grains. The *kumbha* in comparison was probably built by families who were not primarily subsisting through agriculture, but through gathering and hunting, like the Birhors. The *kumbha* then emerges as a contemporary of the *ath-chala,* which was built by agriculturist families, as compared to its own forest-dwelling inhabitants.

Scholars in the late nineteenth century make passing mention of the houses built by Santals at the time. Hunter, for instance, mentions a leaf hut as the only thing a Santal girl expects from her beau at the time of marriage.[22] This is a clear reference to the leaf-covered roof of the *kumbha.* Bodding, a Jesuit priest who pioneered much of early scholarship on the Santal community described the Santal house at the turn of the twentieth century as something very similar to the *kumbha.*[23] He describes the structure as comprising a series of wooden poles with beams tied above. The walls were made of panels of wood strips and branches tied together. Bodding notes, however, that it was increasingly common for families to plaster the walls with clay. This gave the interior spaces much better protection from the elements and made the structure more permanent. He suggested that it was likely that the wooden houses over the next few years will get replaced with mud construction.[24] What is interesting here is not only that Bodding was to prove prophetic, but that his narrative provides a rare chronicle of the time and nature of transformation of Santal houses.

Putting these anecdotes together allows us to string a trajectory of transformation of the domestic architecture of the region. In terms of dominant or commonly built house types, in the late nineteenth century we find the *ath-chala* built by wealthier families or at least those who owned land and earned a significant part of their livelihood from agricultural, while others lived in the *kumbha*. In some of the *kumbha,* families had started adding mud plaster to the walls, which resonated with Bodding's observations. The single internal space of the *kumbha* has the same activities, viz., storing the family's belongings, cooking, and worship, as we would find in the single-room *orak*. In this way, it is likely that the *kumbha* were increasingly transforming into the *orak*. The single-room *orak* over time developed into the larger houses with the yards. In short, over the late nineteenth and early twentieth centuries, the *ath-chala* and the *kumbha* gradually gave way to the mud *orak* as the most common house type in the region.

FROM FOREST TO FIELD AND FACTORY

The period of the late-nineteenth and early twentieth centuries was a time of significant transformation in the Singhbhum region, and indeed, in the Indian subcontinent as a whole. The British East India Company was rapidly bringing kingdoms, chiefdoms and various other areas under control. In his early nineteenth-century history of Singhbhum, K. K. Basu notes that Singhbhum lay in the interstices of various chiefdoms and colonial agencies.[25] To the north and west lay Chotanagpur and to the east were Dalbhum and Manbhum, all of which were under colonial administration. To the south were Mayurbhanj and Keonjhar, which were under a titular king. The landscape of Singhbhum was hilly, thickly forested and home to large numbers of Larka Kols, or the fighting Kols as the colonial administration identified them. Very few rulers, even in the past, attempted to infiltrate the region for the fear of the Kols. In Santal geography, the western part of Singhbhum is known as Mogulbondi, literally meaning Mughal captive.[26] It refers to a story about a Mughal general, who attempted to bring the region under Delhi's rule in the seventeenth or eighteen century, but failed because he was captured by the Larka Kols. Singhbhum as a whole was not part of a kingdom or chiefdom, which meant that fugitives from the neighbouring regions often escaped into the dense forests of the region. There were, however, small chiefdoms such as Seraikela and Kharsawan that were under the rule of landlords. It is not the number but the particular relationship between the landlords, the colonial government and the Adivasis that is significant. The landlords, both in Singhbhum and elsewhere in Chotanagpur were non-Adivasis who had migrated into the region following the Permanent Zamindari Settlement promulgated by the British East India Company in 1790. The Settlement permitted this new class of petty rulers to control stretches of land against the payment of a fixed revenue to the Company. In lieu of this, the landlords were encouraged to clear forests and bring land under cultivation. Much of this clearing was usually carried out by Adivasi labourers. Santals were particularly renowned for their skills in clearing forests and grading land in preparation for paddy cultivation, and large bands moved across the region finding employment as labourers.

The movement of Adivasis across the landscape of Chotanagpur was not necessarily a new development or prompted by colonial rule alone. Adivasi groups migrated across the region since medieval times. This is mythologised in local songs and oral traditions and also supported by ethno-archaeological evidence such as the megalithic grave stones, characteristic of Mundas and Hos, and found in various villages across the region. The present-day inhabitants often belong to other Adivasi and non-Adivasi communities, indicating that the demography changed at some point in the past. This was seen in Bandudih, where an elderly villager showed me a huge stone placed at the entrance of his house. It looked like an ordinary rock but was distinctly different from those found locally. The villager mentioned that this was brought from somewhere else and placed here as per Ho tradition.[27] He was certain that Hos were the original inhabitants of Bandudih but did not know how or when Mundas and Santals came to replace them. In another conversation, Kanshiram Singh offered a reason for why Adivasi families moved from one site of living to another. He suggested that people moved when they felt that a particular site did not 'suit' them.[28] People attribute illnesses, difficult living conditions, or other problems to the displeasure of spirits who reside in a particular place. This fear, according to Singh, was quite a powerful belief and made people move from one place to another. While it is nearly impossible to precisely map the patterns of movement of Adivasi communities, it is certain that families and entire communities were relatively mobile across the region.

The clearing of forests and the conversion of land for agriculture accelerated towards the end of the nineteenth century. Dutta-Majumdar describes this in the Damin-i-Koh, a region to the north of Singhbhum where the colonial government reserved a very large area of fertile forest in the valleys of the Rajmahal Hills.[29] This drew a large number of Santals who eventually cleared the forest and settled as rent paying cultivators of the area. Similarly, indigo plantations emerged in a big way in Bengal and also attracted large numbers of Santals. Spurred by the revenue that agriculture brought in, forests in various parts of Singhbhum, particularly areas which were under the control of landlords, were being cleared. At the same time, the establishment of the iron and steel factory in the village of Kalimati (which later developed into Jamshedpur) created a new locus of movement in the region.

These transformations find correspondence in the gradual shift from the *ath-chala-* and *kumbha*-type houses to the *orak*. In the late nineteenth century, there is increasing agriculture, growing numbers of landlords and increasingly settled agriculturists on the one hand, while bands of Adivasi families are still relatively mobile and moving from place to place in search of livelihoods. The dwellings of the landowning agri-culturist families were likely to be of the *ath-chala* type, while the latter built *kumbha* which was easily built and abandoned when they needed to move to another location. With the colonial government's move to push agriculture in lieu of revenues, more and more Adivasi families became settled as agricultural labourers, if not landowners, as in the case of Damin-i-Koh. As families lived on the same locations for longer periods, it is likely that the *kumbha* was consolidated using mud plaster, as the Birhor families tend to do even today. Bodding's prediction about mud houses, i.e., *orak,* replacing the then current wooden houses, i.e., the *kumbha,* now appears to prophesy not just material architectural change but a wider social and economic shift from forest dwelling to a life of settled agriculture.

From the early twentieth century onwards, agriculture dominates as a primary mode of living in Singhbhum. In the wake of the conversion of forests into agricultural land, new village settlements emerge. Bhagabondi was one such case. Given that it has only *orak*, one can surmise that these had come into currency as the common form of houses of agricultural families. Around this time, the factory in Jamshedpur and its neighbouring areas created a new avenue for employment. Villagers who did not own land or were unable to subsist through agricultural labour in other people's fields, now began to work as labourers in factories and mines. Architecturally, this created a shift as well. In earlier times, when families failed to find subsistence in a particular location they would move elsewhere. Now, they continued to stay in their village, while only the men, and subsequently the women as well, travelled to work as wage labourers and then returned to their village. The mobile form of the *kumbha* was almost rendered irrelevant as families' houses became more permanent, since they now commuted between their places of living and working.

The addition or division of rooms that results in various sizes and configurations of the *orak* also corresponds to these shifts. I discussed earlier that the marriage of a son usually entails the formation of a new household and spatially, when land and resources permit, a new *orak* as well. Prior to the turn of the twentieth century, when bands of families migrated across the landscape, each new site of inhabitation required the building of a new *kumbha*. If a new household was to be set up, a new *kumbha* would be added to the village settlement through mutual agreement between the members of the community. This was particularly enabled by the fact that the occupation of land was governed by the village council and not necessarily owned by a family. By the turn of the century, however, villages had become revenue paying units and families were being associated with particular plots of land as owners or rent payers. Families now lived on the same site over generations. As the families grew, space for building houses became scarce, leading to the subdivision of existing *orak* to accommodate extended families. Villages such as Bandudih are very densely populated today.

One of the reasons why such density exists in Bandudih is because it has a large population of people working in Jamshedpur. From the earliest days of the establishment of the factory, Bandudih was connected to what was then a fledgling industrial centre through a highway. The ease of connectivity led to a much longer history of Adivasis working as labourers in the city while continuing to live in the village. Village houses have divided so intensely over generations that not only are houses shared by extended families, but people have started building away from the *kulhi* and behind other houses. This is almost a contravention of a widely held Santal social practice, where being located directly on the *kulhi* is a register of membership within the community.

CHANGING IN CHANGING TIMES

Within this broad trajectory of architectural transformations there are a host of other details that signal how Adivasi lives were changing. One such detail is the emergence of the enclosed *racha*. As layouts, the *kumbha* and the *ath-chala* have a clear distinction between the yard as a place for socialising and the interior as private space for the family members alone. With the emergence of the *racha* as a space that is within the house yet open to outsiders, it creates an intermediate level in the hierarchy of spaces. In the *ath-chala* or the *kumbha* all outsiders were met with outside the house. The internal *racha*, on the other hand, is a place for meeting people who do not belong to the family but are usually known to them, such as neighbours and other villagers. Complete strangers are not entertained in the *racha*. During fieldwork, most of my preliminary interactions with families took place on the street in the *kulhi racha*, and it was not until the families became more familiar with me that I was invited into the house. The emergence of such an intermediate social space may be symptomatic of a distinction between different types of outsiders (Figure 1.10).

This development may be attributed to the increasing conflict between Adivasis and non–Adivasis in the late nineteenth and the early twentieth centuries. The clearing of forests and control of cultivable

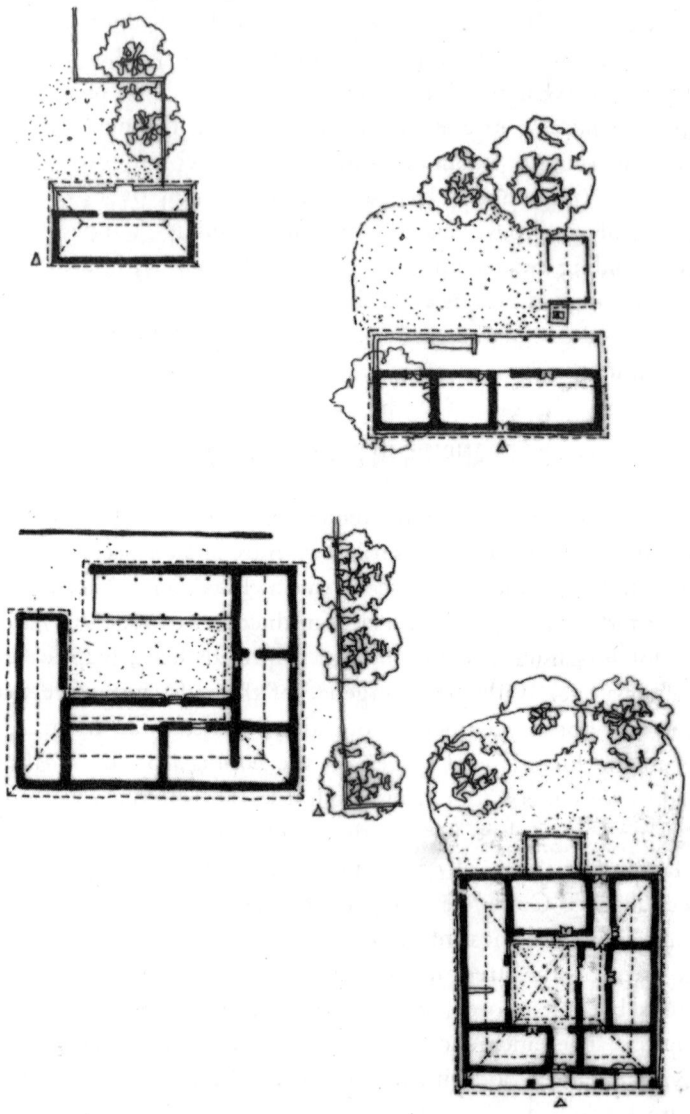

Figure 1.10 *Changing Layout and the Emergence of the* Racha

In the top most *kumbha* or similar house, the *racha* is a simple yard. As more rooms as added to the house, the yard becomes increasingly enclosed.

land by landlords and individual owners led to widespread dispossession and alienation of Adivasi communities. Elsewhere in Chotanagpur, this had already led to rebellions led by leaders such as Birsa Munda.[30] While the Singhbhum region did not see rebellions at the same scale as these movements, a climate of conflict and distrust pervaded the region, particularly over the question of land and resources. Under these circumstances, the definition of outsiders became a complex one.[31] As such village communities had become considerably sedentary, and the relationships between members of the community differentiated into varying degrees of familiarity. Next door neighbours, who may in fact be members of the extended family, have a different threshold of comfort with the family as compared to other villagers or passersby. Second, not only did the villages become dense, but the population of the entire region increased. Additionally, the systems of taxation and revenue meant that various outsiders, such as the officials of landlords and the colonial state, frequented the villages in order to make collections. The world outside the village community was more finely segregated into people with varying levels of comfort and interaction with the Adivasi families. The variations in social interaction resulted in a blurring of the sharp dichotomy between the built spaces and open yards that occurred with the emergence of the internal *racha*.

At the same time, the internal spaces of the houses also underwent a transformation. In the *kumbha* and *ath-chala* houses, activities such as worship, cooking and sheltering of cattle occurred indoors, while in the later *orak* and courtyard layouts, these activities were carried out in different rooms. Compared to designated corners for different activities, the *orak* has discrete spaces for each activity, and as a consequence, a new spatial hierarchy of activities emerge within the layout. This is most clearly seen in the case of the *bhitar* and the cooking areas. Spatially, these rooms constitute the interior core of Santal houses, given that they are always located indoors and are accessible only by family members. As the layouts transformed, these areas remained largely unchanged in terms of norms of access and attributes of the spaces themselves. Across the *ath-chala*, kumbha and the *orak*, only the bhitar and cooking activities are without exception located indoors and visitors are not allowed to access or enter those rooms. What has changed however is the sequence of movement through which these rooms are accessed. In the earlier layouts, these spaces, particularly the *bhitar*, would have physically formed the innermost part of the house. With the *orak* layout however, this is diluted given that all the rooms are, at least formally, organised around the *racha* and thus equally accessible. Only the taboo around access continues to remain, even though the physical configuration no longer suggests the idea.

Against a backdrop of the transforming house, the word *orak* came to refer to both the house and a single room. In the case of rooms with specific activities, *orak* is prefixed with the word that describes whatever takes place in the room. As seen before, the room for cooking is known as *dakal orak,* where *dakal* refers to rice. The entrance vestibule is known as the *duar orak,* where *duar* refers to a door. However, the entire house itself is also referred to as *orak*. The use of the same term is linked to the transformation of Santal dwellings. In the earlier layouts, the dwelling comprised a single volume that was known as *orak*. In the later layouts, though the numbers of individual spaces increased, both the entire house and the spaces contained within it were referred to as *orak*. There is a distinct possibility that the room and house are conceptually conflated in Santal imagination. This conflation is echoed in the ritual practices performed at the entrance of the house. The first task of the day for women in Santal families is to apply a patch of cow dung plaster at the entrance of the house. In the *ath-chala* or *kumbha*, when there was a single entrance into the interior of the house, the application of plaster at that entrance was enough to ritually purify the entire dwelling. Today the practice of applying cow dung continues, except that it is now applied to the entrance leading from the *kulhi* into the *racha*, and also outside the entrances to the various rooms of the house. Given that this gesture of ritual purification is done through the entrance, it also marks the point at which the domestic space of the house must notionally begin. It is interesting then, that the house obviously begins at the front door, but then also begins at the thresholds of the various rooms. The latter is a consequence of the cultural memory of the house as being the distinctive interior space as compared to the outdoors. So in the present-day *orak*, the physical extent of the domestic space, including rooms and the *racha,* is an imaginary one that exists alongside the memory of interiors being the spaces of dwelling.

The practices of demarcating and using the *racha* and the *barge* (backyard garden) further underscore the idea that the transformation of house forms was not absolute, but rather, retained memories of past dwellings and spatial practices. The act of plastering ground surfaces with cow dung remains an important domestic chore. In the past, it was essential for territorial as well as functional reasons. The *racha* had to be distinguished from the rest of the ground, since the enclosure, if it existed at all, would have been a nominal fence. Also, given that many communities lived within or close to forested areas, the ground would have been covered with plants, scrub and fallen leaves. Plastering the ground was a way of keeping the *racha* clear. Over time, these needs and practices intersected with ritual belief and became imbued with ritual significance. In many houses today, the *racha* is clearly defined by rooms on all sides. The floor too, in many houses, is covered with cement. Plastering thus neither serves as a process of marking territory nor is there a functional need to clear the ground. It continues on account of the ritual need to purify the house.

In addition to the plastering of the *racha,* Santal women constantly strive to tidy the house by picking things off the floor and depositing them on higher surfaces such as the eaves of the sloping roofs. Nearly all objects in Santal houses are stored off the ground. Clothes are hung on rope and bamboo swings; brooms, baskets and other such objects are kept on the roof; and agricultural implements are stored in temporary lofts within animal shelters. Combined with efforts made to plaster and clean floors, the sense of the floor in Santal houses is reminiscent of a camp-like environment where the ground is kept clear, as one does not expect the enclosures to keep things protected. Another small gesture that suggests this idea is the protection of the mud stove when not in use. When not in use, the mouth of the *chulha* is kept covered or blocked with dried branches. This is evidently not necessary given that the *chulha* is located indoors, but many women continue this practice. This gesture too is reminiscent of cooking and living in a relatively open area, which offered far less physical protection as compared to the present-day *orak* and where animals had to be kept away from the *chulha*. While these practices are really the minutiae of everyday life, their apparent disjunction with the physical form of present-day habitations reveal deeply rooted cultural memories, and more significantly, hint at the different habitations of the past.

THE TRAJECTORY OF TRANSFORMATION

The change in Santal houses is representative of the wider trajectory of transformation of domestic architecture in the region. The trigger for transformation from the *kumbha* to the *orak* is livelihood and daily sustenance, which are common to communities across the region. Thus, the architectural changes are similar as well. At the same time, there are some specificities with regard to how Santal houses changed. The pace and the moments in which communities shifted from forest dwelling to agriculture is not the same. Through the late nineteenth and early twentieth centuries, different parts of Singhbhum, and indeed Chotanagpur itself came under colonial control at different times. Tracts of forest were cleared at various moments and this affected the local communities at various points in time as well. Further, different Adivasi communities responded differently to the colonial authorities and the changing landscape. In the Damin-i-Koh, for instance, the Rajmahal Hills were demarcated as a reserved land in a move to bring the Paharia down from the hills to cultivate the fertile valleys. The Paharias did not leave their villages and instead, large numbers of Santal families shifted into the region and settled as cultivators. While this is only an anecdote, it does signal that some communities such as the Santals took to cultivation more readily than others. Their houses transformed at corresponding moments as well. This also accounts for variations in the houses within a community. Santal and other Adivasi families in some regions have a longer local history of agriculture and sedentarisation, and they must have shifted to the *orak* earlier than in other places. The point here is that the shift from *kumbha* to *orak* accompanied this gradual shift from a forest dwelling to an agricultural occupation and lifestyle. Since that happened in various places under different circumstances and at different points in time, the changes in domestic architecture were varied as well.

Within this broad trajectory, however, there are cultural specificities at play. I discussed earlier that Munda and Santal houses are divided and expanded with very different approaches to geometry. Munda houses are expanded as and where space is available, while Santal houses are expanded with particular care to maintain the orthogonal geometry and direct approach from the street. Therefore, though the principles of division of the house remain the same, viz., married sons usually set up a separate household, the forms of division or addition of rooms is more rigorously geometrical among Santals than it is among other communities. When rooms get added to Santal houses, they are added in such a way that the *racha* remains a nearly square or rectangular space. New houses are also built such that they are neatly perpendicular to the central *kulhi*. The principle of direct access to the *kulhi* is spatially enforced. Munda house clusters on the other hand tend to have more varied forms. Compared to the Santal *racha* that lies usually within or behind the *orak*, Munda houses have yards in front, on the side and at the back, depending on the location of the rooms. The addition of new rooms is determined more by the contingencies of the immediately available space and needs of the family than with overt considerations regarding geometry.

Even within a house, differences in religious and domestic practice lead to variations in the internal layout of the houses. Mundas, as a group, are relatively more Hinduised in comparison to other Adivasis. Munda families have a *bhitar* but they worship two different kinds of deities, spirits from the Munda pantheon similar to Santal spirits and also Hindu gods and goddesses. Interestingly, the two are not worshipped together or in the same space. Kanshiram Singh pointed out that the two deities are different and require different kinds of propitiation, and so they keep the two places of worship separate. In Mahato houses, the place for prayers is similar to shrines or *puja* (worship) rooms in Hindu houses, with a series of idols or images displayed against a wall and where the family lights oil lamps and incense and chants prayers. Mahatos also do not have taboos around allowing outsiders to view or access these rooms. The point here is that most communities have a space dedicated to worship, but its location within the layout and the rules around access vary according to the religious practice of that particular community. A similar pattern is evident across the communities. Being primarily agricultural, their domestic spaces constitute a similar set of activities, while the cultural differences in kinship structure, religious practice, and taboos associated with various domestic activities, create different internal configurations and patterns of everyday inhabitation.

It is tempting to label the regional trajectory of transformation as the schematic model of domestic architecture and to posit the cultural specificities as variations. The picture, however, is neither so simple nor so straightforward. I discussed earlier that the trajectory of architectural change across Singhbhum was neither singular in terms of how it took place nor can it be explicated in terms of a uniform set of determinants. Rather, what we find is a variegated landscape of families, communities, livelihoods, and historical forces. Houses in each instance have emerged in the interplay of these factors as well as the contingencies of time and place. The fact that houses share many points of similarity as well as difference, is linked to the larger reality of Adivasi history. Rather than being discrete and internally homogenous groups, Adivasi communities have a number of overlapping social, cultural and economic characteristics, and yet have distinctive local identities and histories.

Chapter 2

Materials and Making

According to most villagers, building the *orak* was a fairly simple matter. The walls are made with mud, a wooden roof is added, and the house is ready. They were amused by my questions regarding construction processes. Why should I, a city dweller who had seen the permanent and much better brick and concrete structures, be interested in mud houses? These were after all ordinary, poor people's houses, they said. Their self-deprecation notwithstanding, Santal houses are exceptionally produced architectural works. They are characterised by very precise construction: the walls have sharp edges and smooth surfaces; floors and other ground surfaces are neatly plastered; and the roofs are often elaborate with complex geometries. What is particularly interesting is that though most communities across the Singhbhum region, and indeed the Chotanagpur Plateau at large, use the same palette of materials and construction technology, Santal houses display more precise craftsmanship, decoration, and more routine care and maintenance. In light of the previous chapter, what is even more intriguing is that the houses were not always built like this. When the wooden *kumbha* gave way to the present-day mud *orak* the shift in material naturally entailed a shift in how these houses were made, since building in wood clearly requires a very different set of resources, knowledge, and skills. It took many conversations to unravel the details of how these houses are made. What emerged eventually was a fairly complex picture involving a number of stages, materials, and specific skills and negotiations around material, labour and resources.

FROM WOOD TO MUD

The physical structure of the *orak* has three key parts: the foundation, walls, and the roof. Construction begins with digging the foundation. The profile of the room to be built is marked on the ground using pegs. Men, or boys old enough to work, begin digging. *Murrum mati,* the local clayey soil is very hard and dense when dry, so they begin by scratching the surface of the ground. They then flood it with water and leave it to soak overnight and then dig to the required depth, usually two to three feet below the ground depending on the compactness of the soil. Depending on the region, the soil may have rocks of varying sizes or smaller stones and finer clay. Whatever the material, it is used to build the walls and if more is required, it is dug from one corner of the family's own backyard, provided it is large enough. If a large amount of stone is available, it is broken to smaller pieces that can be handled by the person who will lay it. The stones provide the bulk, while *murrum* is required as mortar. If the material is primarily *murrum*, small pieces of stone are added. These will eventually give the wall additional strength.

The *murrum* requires preparation before it can be used. It needs to be soaked and kneaded repeatedly in order to bring out its cohesive properties. Men dig a pit and pile the *murrum* into it. It is then soaked with water and kneaded by stamping it with their feet. This is repeated a few times, after which it is ready. Loads of the *murrum* are carried to the building site. First the foundation trench is filled and tightly packed with soil. After this has rested for a day, the rest of the wall is raised. Large rounds or cobs are placed and shaped by hand into the profile of the wall along the entire length, creating a layer approximately 30 centimetres in thickness. This is left to dry, following which the next layer is added. This continues to a height of about two metres, which is as far as a person can reach with a stool or something else to stand on. In case of stone, the pieces of stone are interspersed with *murrum* and the foundations and walls are built up in a similar manner. This entire process from preparing *murrum* to gathering stone and building the wall is usually carried out by men since Santals traditionally have taboos around women digging soil.[32]

The roof is constructed by men alone. Santals believe that they co-habit this world with a number of spirits, deities from the Santal pantheon as well as spirits of deceased ancestors. These spirits reside in the house and are easily angered or upset by the inappropriate presence of women. To allow a woman to build the roof would require her to stand at that level, which is considered the equivalent of standing above the heads of the deities. So, women do not get involved in the construction of the roof at all. The first part following the completion of the wall is the laying of the primary structural elements of the roof, viz., the ridge beam, which supports all the rafters and is laid along the length in the centre of the room (Figure 2.1). The walls at the two ends may need to be raised in order to support the ridge beam at the required height. The ridge beam may be nestled within the wall in order to ensure it stays in place. In the case of smaller rooms, a single length of wood is sufficient. Most rooms are usually longer, and two or more pieces are combined to provide the required length. The end part of the beams are cut in half and then placed on each other.

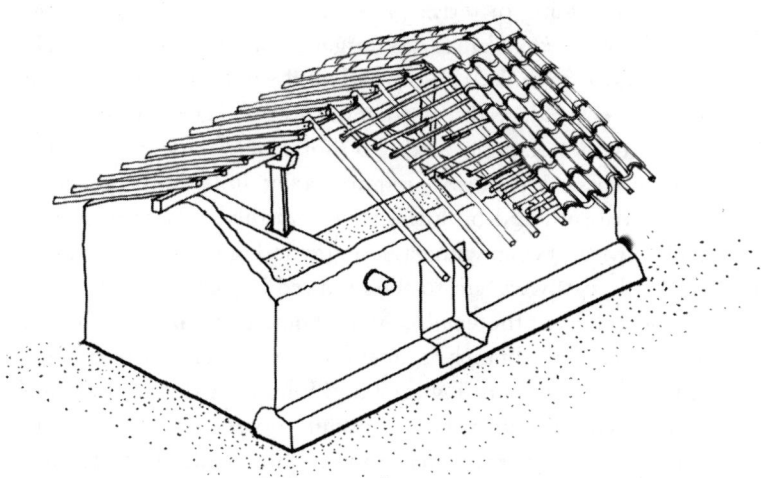

Figure 2.1 *Roof Structure of the* Orak

Note the sequence of members from beam and post prop, ridge beam, rafters, battens, and finally the roofing material of cylindrical clay tiles.

This requires support to stay in place, and so the joint is propped up by a small post which stands on a beam supported on the mud walls. Next, the rafters are added. They are single lengths of wood that are placed at an incline, supported by the ridge beam on the top and the mud walls at the lower end. Rafters placed on either side of the ridge beam create the basic profile of the sloping roof, which is characteristic of the *orak*. In order to prevent the rafters from sliding off, they are pinned to each other above the ridge beam. Apart from this, the weight of the roofing material, whether thatch or clay tiles, also helps keep the rafters in place. Battens, which are thin strips of wood or bamboo, are now tied to the rafters and provide the anchor for the roofing materials. Thatch requires battens placed close together, while in the case of tiles, the distance between two battens is decided by the length of the tile. Finally, the roof is complete and only the plastering and painting of the walls remains, which is usually carried out by women.

The construction of the *orak* may take between three weeks to three months, depending upon the number of hands working on it and the availability of building materials. The *kumbha* in contrast can be built in two days. Since *kumbha* are no longer built today, the time taken and the process as a whole are estimated on the basis of temporary sheds that the villagers build. As discussed in the previous chapter, these sheds together with the example of the Birhor *kumbha* are similar to the *kumbha* in the past. The *kumbha* required a few holes in the ground by way of foundations, and both the walls and the roofs were made of wood. The process began with gathering wood of required lengths and sizes. Vertical posts were cut to the required height, which would be equal to the height of the *kumbha* itself. These posts had a forked end, devised from naturally branched junctions of wood and used to support the beams that rested on it (Figure 2.2). Holes were dug in the ground and the posts inserted into them. Bodding notes that a typical house would have nine posts arranged in rows of three with the middle posts being higher.[33] Once the posts were in place, lengths of wood were cut to be used as beams. Beams were placed on each row of posts, nestled within the forked ends or simply tied using rope. The beam along the middle row of posts became the ridge beam, and the highest point of the sloping roof, while the beams on the other two rows of

Figure 2.2 *Structure of the* kumbha

posts form the eaves or the lower edge of the roof. After this, cross beams were placed, resting on the eaves beam at one end and tied to the middle row of posts on the other. Then came the rafters, made of smaller lengths of wood and supported by the ridge and eaves beams respectively. As in the case of the *orak* roof, rafters were tied to each beam to prevent them from sliding down the slope. A layer of battens is now added. These are thin strips meant primarily to hold the roofing material in place. One batten is tied near the ridge end of the slope, one in the middle and one towards the eaves end. The basic structure of the house is now complete and only the walls and roof surfaces remain to be added. These are known as *jhanti* and are assembled using thin pieces of wood and leafy branches, twigs and other such material as the infill. To make the panels, the strips are laid on the ground in two or three lines. The infill material is then placed on the strips, perpendicular to it if the material being used is sticks. A second layer of strips is placed above this and the whole assemblage is tied together to form a sandwiched panel. These panels are then tied to the posts and become the walls. The roof panel is similarly made, comprising layers of leaves, thatch, twigs, or a combination of these, tied together to create a thicker panel. This is tied securely to the battens to prevent it from being blown away by the strong winds that blow during rains and thunder storms in the region.

TRIGGERS OF TRANSFORMATION

One of the most obvious differences between the *kumbha* and the *orak* is that of building material. The *orak* is built with *murrum mati* while the *kumbha* is made of wood. In the nineteenth century, Singhbhum and most of the Chotanagpur Plateau was covered in dense forests, and wood was plentiful. As Santals and other Adivasis migrated from one location to the other, they found forests where they could temporarily make their homes and sufficient wood to make them with. Extrapolating from the patterns of gathering wood today, Adivasis, usually women and children, went into the forest some distance away from where they lived. They cut lengths of thick wood with branched ends required for the vertical posts, and thinner wood for the beams and rafters of the roof. They then collected a number of very thin branches together with the leaves for the *jhanti* panels. They also stripped tree bark and gathered creepers or plant fibres that were used for tying the various parts of the *kumbha* structure together. While in the forest, the fibres are used to tie the bundles of wood in order to carry it back to the dwelling site on their heads. In terms of tools, a sickle sufficed for this entire process. Even on the building site, the sickle or a sharp knife was enough for cutting the wood into necessary lengths and removing any protrusions. The fact that the structure was mostly tied together meant that no further elaborate carpentry was required to build the house. Once all this material was on the site, it was tied together and assembled.

One of the key structural changes that occurred during this time was a system of taxation of land, which fundamentally altered Adivasi and non-Adivasi people's relationships to their environment. Politically, in the nineteenth and early twentieth centuries, colonial rule was firmly established across the Indian subcontinent. Eastern India, particularly the modern-day states of Bengal, Bihar, Jharkhand and Orissa, were among the first large areas to come under colonial control and be subject to taxes payable on land.[34] This in turn required the identification of individuals with particular parcels of land, in order that the revenues and the payees could be fixed. These legislations were applied not only to agricultural land but also to pastures and forests, which directly affected rural families, who drew a significant part of their subsistence from these resources. In Singhbhum and Chotanagpur this led to systematic disruption of Adivasi migrations and settlement in the forests, leading to well-known conflicts such as the one led by Birsa Munda in the regions around Ranchi, and the Santal rebellion in the north. On a day-to-day basis, Adivasi access to the forests was restricted, and in some cases, prohibited altogether. There were strict penalties for those 'illegally' gathering wood. Yet, complete avoidance of the forests was not possible because most Adivasi families, even those who owned or cultivated land, procured essentials such as wood, for use as fuel and for building, and gathered fruits, edible plants and other organic material from the forests. The forests were also an important site for rituals and hunting, which was and continues to be an important part of the annual Adivasi calendar. While some degree of dependence and therefore the practices of forest gathering persisted, it did transform in significant ways.

The roof of the house, irrespective of type, continues to be constructed out of wood. However, the impact of reducing access to the raw material is discernible. The oldest houses have thick logs used as beams. These range from 20 to 30 cm in diameter and are placed on the walls forming the first layer of support for the roof. Beams with a diameter between 10 and 15 cm were used in other parts of the roof. In newer houses, generally thinner beams are used and these are square or rectangular in sectional profile. Each of these sizes and shapes reveal the source: the thickest beams nearly always belong to a time when wood was plentiful and easily available, while the thinner beams indicate reduced availability. A further distinction can be made based on the shape of the wooden section. Wood procured from forests is usually rounded and minimally worked on, while the rectangular sections are commercially purchased timber, which villagers resort to when wood is not available at all in the vicinity of the village. In this way, the wooden roof members are almost an index of reducing access to wood.

Restricted access to forests is a legacy that marks villagers' relationship to forests even today. Wood remains an important, and often sole, source of fuel and is required for the roof, fences and other temporary constructions. I asked the villagers about where they got the wood from and in most cases, across the region, the answers were largely non-committal. Villagers do foray into the forest, since women armed with a sickle and carrying loads of wood on their heads are a common sight. Yet, they hesitate to discuss this. In one village, during my first visit, I was being shown around the surrounding areas and we came across a group of three women clearly returning from the forest. They spotted me and stopped in their tracks. A brief conversation between the women and my guide ensued. My guide later mentioned that the women wanted to know if I was a forest official. They were fearful since they legally have limited access to the forests, and encounters with State officials are marked with fear and suspicion. In every village, people were reluctant to answer what according to me were rather benign questions about gathering wood. In the few instances that I did accompany women and children, they continued with their work of cutting thin branches and small pieces of wood but were watchful and clearly unhappy about me asking questions and taking photographs. Considering how widespread this fear is and the fact that wood remains a basic requirement for cooking and other domestic activities, the forest is clearly a contested terrain. Thinking back to the late nineteenth century, when these restrictions first came into place and trespassing was met with severe penalties, cutting lengths of wood for construction must have been nearly impossible for most villagers.

Alongside the restriction of access to forests, there was a widespread increase in settled agriculture through the nineteenth century. Prior to this period, Adivasi groups such as the Hos had practised shifting cultivation, a semi-permanent form of agriculture suited to the migratory nature of Adivasi families of this time. Families cleared a part of the forest and grew crops such as millet and mustard, before moving on to another site.[35] Under colonial rule, the area under cultivation increased manifold, leading to substantial revenues for the government.[36] This expansion was facilitated by the control of forests by the State which restricted Adivasi migration, introduction of railways which provided an impetus for grain export, and the influx of non-Adivasis which provided new cohorts of peasant labourers. Under their combined influence, Adivasi families were gradually co-opted into the ecology and economy of settled agriculture. Of the many Adivasi communities, it was Santals who, as O'Malley noted, were particularly sought as labourers because they were 'industrious people who required only good treatment to make them useful and profitable ryots', i.e., agricultural labourers.[37] Santal families settled in large numbers across the region, such as those who moved into the valleys of the Rajmahal Hills. In terms of building practices, the process of sedentarisation meant that families were now living on the same site for longer periods. The early signs of how this changed the *kumbha* can be seen in the houses of the Birhor families who have been living on the same site for long periods. The initial structure is made of wood, but they soon begin to plaster the *jhanti* walls of the *kumbha* with mud. Initially, the part closest to the ground is plastered, and over time the entire wall gets covered. This not only makes the wall less porous, but also makes the house more permanent, since the wood is no longer exposed and therefore does not rot. Considering that wood had, by this time, become a scarce resource, it was judicious to use mud plaster as a way of increasing the life span of the wooden structure.

Around this time, the new legislations around land, particularly those of taxation, led to the idea of private property. This was a complex system underpinned by varied ideas and modes of ownership, use, and therefore the onus of tax. Tuckey notes various kinds of tenancies for both agricultural and non-agricultural lands, which required the occupiers of the land to pay revenues associated with each type.[38] The system was applied on homestead plots as well, i.e., revenue was collected not just on cultivated land, but also on the plots where villagers built their houses. This was because homestead plots were legally considered part of the agricultural holdings and therefore assessed for rent. By the early twentieth century, in many villages around and to the south of Jamshedpur, large numbers of villagers were residing on plots that were listed as non-agricultural. This was spurred by the increase in population due to industries, which resulted in more in-migration and also people leaving agricultural work for industrial wage labour. In such cases, the non-agricultural tenants were given a different kind of land deed and the rents were assessed differently. Irrespective of the structures of ownership and use, or rent, what this led to was the identification of particular parcels of land with individuals who had some rights over it, whether as owner, renter or cultivator. In terms of house building, this not only meant that families were now living on the same site for longer periods, generations in some cases, but also that they could now extract *murrum mati* for construction from their own plots. Combined with the decreased access to wood, within a few decades, *murrum* replaced wood as the primary building material.

Changing resource networks and access continue to influence building practices. Bricks are a relatively recent addition to the reper-toire of commonly used materials in rural areas. Not only are they used with *murrum* plaster as in the case of stones, as mentioned earlier, but, where people can afford it, entire structures are built in brick. One of the factors leading to increased brick usage is the increasing density of villages, which has meant that people have smaller backyards and therefore reduced area for digging *murrum*. Additionally, villagers in most areas have converted their fields into kilns and brick is now widely manufactured. In Bhagabondhi, for instance, bricks are pro-duced in two areas within the village which employ villagers, and the wages from this work are used to buy bricks for construction. Similar changes are taking place with cement being used in addition to or as replacement of mud for plastering walls and floors, and in the case of roofing materials, roofing sheets are increasingly used in place of burnt clay tiles.

CHANGING LABOUR CONDITIONS

The change in building material entailed a change in labour as well. The *orak* requires people for digging, preparing the *murrum*, breaking stone, building the walls, placing the structure of the roof, laying the roofing material, and finally plastering and painting the walls. The roofs are built by men alone and the plastering and painting of the walls are exclusively the domain of women. The other processes are done both by men and women, in spite of taboos against women digging the ground and angering the spirits of the Santal pantheon. In case of the *kumbha*, it is difficult to ascertain any clear divisions in construction, but it is likely that taboos against women digging the ground, climbing the roof, or other restrictions in connection with the presence of spirits, may have existed. What is also likely is that gender roles in construction were contingent upon various factors. Even taboos, which earlier scholars noted as having considerable social currency, for instance, are not absolute but negotiated under certain circumstances. In Haudah,

I observed a young woman digging and breaking large rocks from her backyard and transporting it to the site where she was building a room. Seeing her work alone every day, I asked my guide, who was her neighbour, about the taboos around women digging the earth. She said the family comprised the couple living together with the husband's two younger siblings, who both attended school. During the day, the husband and his siblings were away at work and school respectively. They needed a room urgently and so the young woman was carrying out construction work on her own. It would probably take her three months to complete it. She spent the afternoons digging her backyard for rocks and *murrum*. She then broke the rocks into smaller pieces suitable for use in the wall and dug and readied the *murrum* by soaking and kneading. Then as and when she and her family members could manage the time, they built the wall. My guide concluded that circumstances were difficult, and there was no choice for families, but to do such things (i.e., ignore the taboo).

This was a clear instance of wage labour as a mode of employment impacting the building practices and the beliefs associated with it. Wage labour is not a recent phenomenon in these parts. Adivasis were already employed as agricultural labourers since the nineteenth century, which led to mud becoming the common material for building the *orak*. Industrial wage labour however produced another shift. Industrialisation probably began in Singhbhum in the mid-nineteenth century.[39] The Bengal-Nagpur Railway line was laid in these parts a few decades later. By the early twentieth century, the iron and steel factory was being built in Jamshedpur, and together with a number of allied factories, industrialisation was soon in full swing. Local Adivasi men and women comprised the labour force in all these developments. An elderly villager in Haudah recollected how information about employment opportunities spread and people migrated for work. He remembers hearing from his grandfather that some men came to the village one day and talked about a 'steel factory' being built across the river (referring to the River Kharkhai that runs southwest of Jamshedpur; Haudah lies further south of the river). They needed men to work on the site and the pay would help the families eat better. Haudah was located in a relatively arid and dry part of the Singhbhum. Far from the river valleys, it had less water and only one crop of paddy in the year. A few men decided to go along and see if they could find work. They set off at four o'clock in the morning walking through the dense forest, armed with a *mashal* (a fire torch) and knives to protect themselves from animals. It was a four-hour trek and they arrived on the construction site at eight o'clock. The man who had brought the information to the village introduced them to the contractor, who hired the men. They worked until sundown, when they set off on the trek back arriving at the village past nine o'clock. Next morning, the group set off again to work and this continued. If the work provided more sustenance than the men managed from paddy cultivation, they moved into the temporary settlements that had emerged in the peripheries of the construction site and the city.

When they worked as agricultural labourers, the villagers had a break in the annual cycle between harvest, which was towards the end of December, and the monsoons in June when the next paddy season started. Most house-building activities took place between January and April, just before the searing hot summer began. Also, most farmers grew enough paddy to sustain them through the year and so these months were devoted to other activities. With wage labour, however, there was no break. There were also no surpluses since most families needed to earn money regularly in order to sustain themselves. The lack of time among family members for building, combined with the availability of cash, introduced the possibility of hiring labourers to carry out construction. Based on these present-day arrangements and the fact that many villagers were earning cash wages since the early twentieth century, it is plausible that house building was historically managed through the practice of hiring labour, fellow villagers even, in exchange for monetary payment.

Possibilities of wage labour were not only occurring outside the village in factory sites such as Jamshedpur, but within the villages and their vicinity as well. The brick kilns and stone quarries that dot the hinterlands of Jamshedpur, were fuelled to a large extent by the intensive industrial building activity that went on for the first few decades of the twentieth century. These were set up by villagers within their fields or by private contractors licensed by the state to carry out production in the surrounding areas. This development had the dual impact of providing wage labour opportunities to villagers, while also offering stone and particularly brick as a construction material. In Bhagabondhi, for instance, the Mahato Tola (one of the four neighbourhoods that make up the village precinct) has a brick kiln. This provides employment to many villagers, while also selling damaged bricks to the villagers at low prices. Additionally, one of the villagers owns a truck that is hired to transport the bricks from the kiln to the dwelling construction sites. In Bandudih, a kiln was newly established during my period of visiting the villagers and a number of villagers were seeking employment in the kiln. It offered the villagers a local site of employment and also made bricks easily available in the village.

ROOFING: A BRIEF SUMMARY OF THE ECOLOGY OF MATERIALS AND LABOUR

Building materials and their use clearly lies in the intersection of availability, access, labour within the family, or cash for purchasing alternatives. While this is a complex set of interconnected factors and processes, it becomes clearly comprehensible in the case of roofing material. Roofing material refers to the final covering that is placed above the wooden supports of the roof. Different kinds of roofing materials are used by the villagers: thatch, made of paddy straw; baked clay tiles, which are either cylindrical and known as *khapra* or rectangular and locally known as *tali*; asbestos-cement roofing sheets and galvanised iron or GI sheets. Of these, thatch is the oldest form of roofing. The *kumbha* were always covered in leaf thatch. Bodding describes Santals in the past preferring the *sauri* grass, which grew in abundance in the forests in the region.[40] By the early twentieth century, with the spread of agricultural practices, people shifted to paddy straw as a thatching material. Bundles of straw were placed on the battens and stitched together using rope and custom-made needles. After three or four layers of thatch, the roof was between 30 and 40 cm in thickness, sufficient to protect the interiors from the heavy rains. Depending on the quality of the thatch and the workmanship, such a roof lasted two to three years, after which new thatch had to be laid on (Figure 2.3).

Figure 2.3 *Making a Roof*

Thatch today, is usually used by poorer families or as a temporary roofing material before tiles or sheets are procured and placed. Families generally aim to roof their houses with the best roofing materials they can afford, and on those grounds, thatch is the least preferred material. This is because though it is the most easily available and can be procured every year after the paddy harvest, thatch is labour-intensive and time-consuming to lay on and also needs replacement every two or three years. Further, for straw to be used as roofing, it needs to be strong and have sufficient length, which is possible only with particular kinds of long-leaved paddy. The use of fertilisers in recent years has resulted in straw becoming brittle and unsuitable for use as thatch.[41] The last consideration affecting the use of paddy, is the balance between using straw as fodder for cattle vis-à-vis its use as roofing. Since most paddy cultivating families keep a few cattle, they need to ensure that they have sufficient fodder, since grazing alone is rarely sufficient to feed the animals. Thatching the roof every two to three years seriously depletes the family's stock of fodder. Given these changes in quality and other conflicting demands of procurement, use, and maintenance, villagers prefer to use tiles or roofing sheets, if they can afford it.

Burnt clay tiles, both *khapra* (cylindrical tiles) and *tali* (rectangular tiles), are preferred over thatch since they have a longer life. Over time, they have become the most common roofing materials used in the rural areas of Singhbhum. Today, both types are commercially produced, but in the past, *khapra* were made by specially commissioned potters, and made as per the specific requirements of the house. Though rare today, one family in Haudah was renovating the roof of their house and hired two potters to make the required *khapra*. The potters had travelled from Gaya district in Bihar. They were farmers themselves but travelled in the Seraikela region during the non-agricultural season and made *khapra* for Adivasi families, when hired to do so. The process began with the potters estimating the number of *khapra* required for the size of the house, the amount of clay for making the *khapra,* the wood required for firing the completed tiles, and their own charges. If the family found the estimates and charges to be acceptable, the potters started work.

Family members were involved in various stages of preparation, while the potters were responsible for shaping the tiles on their wheels and organising the firing. The family members first procured clay from a dried pond bed in the vicinity of the village. This clay is the same *murrum* that is used for building walls but it is required to be finer since the *khapra* are shaped on a potter's wheel. For this reason, only the top layer of *murrum* from the pond or riverbeds is used. The backyard and courtyard of the house being renovated, become the site of work for the duration of the activity. A pit was dug and sacks of clay were emptied into it. This was flooded with water and the clay left to soak for approximately eight hours (Figure 2.4). More water was added as the clay appeared to dry out. The wet clay was removed and kneaded thoroughly, similar to the process followed for preparing the *murrum* for building walls (Figure 2.5). After the clay has been kneaded three or four times, smaller lumps of clay are formed and kneaded by hand. This removes any small stones and pebbles, which if left behind can disrupt the shaping of the tile on the potter's wheel. It was then passed to the potters. Groups of two or three young boys and men took turns kneading the clay to ensure that the potters had an uninterrupted supply of material to work with. The two potters then set to work and shaped the clay into hollow cylinders. The cylinders are narrow at one end and slightly wider at the other end. These were set out to dry in the sun, and when nearly dry, they were split in half to create the

Figure 2.4 *Soaking* Murrum

half-cylinder shape that is characteristic of the *khapra*. When all the tiles were dried and ready, the entire lot was fired. Nearly 7,000 *khapra* were produced in this manner, with each potter shaping between 700 and 900 tiles each day. The entire process involved nearly two weeks of constant work for both the potters and the entire family.

Figure 2.5 *Kneading Clay for Making* Khapra

These tiles are larger in size, thicker, and stronger than commercially available tiles. According to the potters and as endorsed by the family, these tiles would last three or four decades. Yet, this practice is rapidly declining due to a number of reasons. First, the preparations involve the entire extended family (two men, their wives and sons) as in the case above. In recent times, for families with fewer members or where some members work for daily wages, it is impossible to gather enough people to support the project. In earlier times, with more families working primarily in agriculture, villagers may have also invited their neighbours and friends to help with this work. Increasingly, however, most families in the villages are occupied with wage labour, where there is no natural break in the cycle of work, and younger adults and children are busy in school. In some cases, other members of the village community may participate in building, in exchange for wages, but that will increase the total expenditure for the family concerned. A second factor is the time involved, since it takes more than two weeks for the production to be completed. Wage labourers miss days of work and thus lose their daily earnings as well. Finally, resources required for the making of *khapra* are increasingly scarce; both fine *murrum* and wood for firing the tiles are now difficult to obtain from the vicinity of villages. Compared to the *murrum* for walls that is obtained from people's backyards, *murrum* for *khapra* and firewood are both collected from common village resources such as ponds and forests, since the homestead plot will not suffice. With increasing village densities and many more claimants to these resources, these places can no longer provide *murrum* and wood as required by the villagers. Under these circumstances, it is simply more convenient for villagers to buy *khapra*, even if it is of a poorer quality and may need to be replaced sooner than commissioned tiles.

The logic that underpins these choices and negotiations is similar to that which animates the larger ecology of building materials and practices. The availability and use of thatch, mud, or wood is linked to a family's own agricultural practice and property or to village commons. When these sources or modes of access are interrupted, they turn to other materials which need to be purchased using cash. Cash becomes available only when villagers work for wages, which in turn affects the possibility of families building anything themselves. When they work for wages, families also need to hire labour to build on their behalf. The construction of a house, in this way, gets entangled within the network of resources, livelihood, and labour.

Chapter 3

Of Technology and Memory

When construction material changed from wood to *murrum*, it was not a simple replacement of one building material with another. It was accompanied by a complete change in construction process, and therefore a transformation of technological skills, tools, and knowledge. Most Adivasi families built wooden *kumbha* until the late nineteenth century and most families had shifted to the mud *orak* by the mid-twentieth century. Some vestiges of the *kumbha* in the form of wooden sheds or fences persisted, but the building material most commonly in use was clearly *murrum*. This widespread shift raises a number of crucial questions. For instance, how did Adivasi families become familiar with the techniques and tools required for building in mud? How did they negotiate the very different properties of this new material? Which parts of the house changed first and how? These questions are particularly significant because Adivasi technology, like many indigenous building practices, is common rather than specialised knowledge. This means that most people have the skills and technical abilities required to construct their own house. When a region witnesses widespread transformation, the skills and knowledge systems of most resident individuals and communities undergo change. Specialised builders in all parts of the world acquire their skills and knowledge through apprenticeship or systems of training and knowledge transfer. Over time and with each building project, they develop their expertise and innovate in relation to the contingencies of need and context. In comparison, indigenous builders such as the Adivasis build occasionally and typically improvise with the resources available at a given point in time.

Improvisation as a mode of building extends the idea of technology as more than a consistent mechanical skill. What we find when we examine different houses and processes of construction is not a uniform collective knowledge but varied choices and negotiations by individual builders within a shifting landscape of inhabitation. This kind of technology needs to be understood in two ways: first, in terms of the mechanics of the construction process which comprises the basic principles of putting a building together. Considering the similarities of building form across the region, technical concepts such as strength and stability are clearly the same. The other dimension of indigenous technology is the operational logic of the builder, i.e., the considered response of the builder to the context in which they dwell or intend to dwell. Again, there are patterns observed in the kinds of technology improvisations across Singhbhum, which suggest clear correlations between individual technological practice and the contingencies of time and place that result in certain responses. In other words, even though Adivasi technology is not a singular body of systematic knowledge, there are commonalities in form and techniques of making, which inherently emerge from shared contextual triggers.

SITES AND PROCESSES OF CHANGE

The walls of the *kumbha* were the first site of significant change. It began when agricultural labourers plastered the *jhanti* walls of the *kumbha* with *murrum mati* in order to make it more robust. In the mid-nineteenth century, *murrum* was already commonly used to plaster the interior floors and exterior yards of houses, irrespective of type. Additionally, the *ath-chala* house belonging to the landowning elite across the region was built entirely out of *murrum*. Since Adivasi families were employed by the landowners, they are likely to have helped build the walls, carry out repairs, prepare wood for building the roof and laid thatch or roofing tiles. In this way, most families developed a degree of familiarity with the process of mud construction. Somewhere in the course of having settled in one place for a period of time, when families needed to add a room to their existing house, they built a mud *orak*. Based on their experiences of seeing or building the *ath-chala* and their familiarity with *murrum* plaster, they were able to prepare *murrum*, i.e.,

Figure 3.1 Jhanti *Walls and Roof as Seen in the* kumbha

soak and knead it to form cobs for building the wall. This exposure also familiarised them with the structural logic of building a mud wall. The earlier *jhanti* walls were framed panels that were assembled and tied to the poles of the house (Figure 3.1). Mud walls are masonry structures that attain stability through mass. The principles involved

Figure 3.2 Murrum *Walls under Construction*

are simple: that the wall being built needs to be thick enough to support the layer that comes above it (Figure 3.2). This understanding came from the *ath-chala* but also from the fact that as agriculturists, most Adivasis worked extensively with grading land and levelling the ground for paddy cultivation. This led to a familiarity with local soils, which enabled them to build *murrum* walls. In short, Adivasi villagers who had taken to agriculture as many Santals did, developed sufficient skills and exposure for practising mud construction. While the extent of skill and knowledge is difficult to determine, we can safely conjecture that they could build four solid walls required to create an *orak*. We can also conjecture that until this point, the *kumbha* was usually a single room and as a first step, families were primarily replacing the *jhanti* walls of the *kumbha* with the more permanent mud walls. It is likely, therefore, that the early *orak,* in spite of the obvious material and structural differences, was tectonically similar to the *kumbha*.

The *ath-chala* was an obvious point of reference for the *orak* but there was a key difference in the height of the walls. The *ath-chala* walls were higher, at least in the central space, to allow a usable verandah—usable referring to a person being able to stand inside—to be built all around its sides. The *orak* walls, on the other hand, were built to a height ranging from 1.5 to 2 meters. While one reason for this difference may be the amount of *murrum* that the family is able to extract, the other is rooted in the process of construction. Since each layer of the wall is built by hand, the walls are built up as far as the builder can reach. For the final layer, the builder climbs on the wall and a helper passes the cobs from below. In case of the central *ath-chala* walls, the builders used additional support possibly in the form of a wooden step or ladder. This however requires additional resources, both *murrum* for the longer wall and wood for making the supports. Considering the resource-constrained circumstances of most families, building the walls as high as they can without additional support was often the only possibility. The height of the wall was a concern also from the point of view of recurring repairs and maintenance. The walls are plastered and painted each year after the monsoons. So the stool or ladder required to access the top of the walls was a recurring requirement. This small detail signals the simple yet significant fact that resources were constrained for most Adivasi families. The negotiations between material availability and the needs of dwelling was, and continues to be, a factor that influences construction. Further, the idea of negotiations operated at multiple levels. At the scale of the region, changing equations of access to resources was transforming domestic architecture. At the level of families, access to stone, *murrum* or wood determined the specifics of how much and what they could build.

The method of building the roof continued to be similar in the *orak* as it was in the *kumbha*. It sloped on two sides from a central ridge beam to the eaves and was covered with rafters, battens and roofing material. The roof comprised three key parts: the primary layer of beams which gave the roof its basic profile and support, then the secondary layer made of rafters and battens which supported the roofing material, which was the final covering layer. The beams and rafters were made of a length of wood, while the battens were made of wood, cane or bamboo strips depending on their availability. The basic principle of building the roof, both at the level of the primary and the secondary layers, was that the lengths of wood had to be horizontally supported at two ends.

The most basic *kumbha* had three rows with three posts in each row, across which the roof structure was supported. The central row was taller than the poles on either side to create slopes of the roof. Beams were tied across the taller posts to form the ridge beam and along the smaller posts to form the eaves. The beams were approximately 2 metres in length, which is what was available from the forests in the vicinity of the villages. Since they had to be tied to the posts, the posts were placed not more than two metres apart. In this way, the length of the wood available as beams became the determinant of the length of the house. Houses were usually built with at least two rows of posts, and so were at least four metres in length. If more interior space was required, another row of posts was added and the length increased to approximately 6 metres. The width of the house was similarly limited by the length of the rafters, though in this case, there was no possibility for extension. The rafters were also single lengths of wood tied to the ridge beams at one end and to the eaves at the other. Since there was no intermediate support below the rafters, it was not possible to join two pieces of wood to increase the length. The width of the house was thus only as much as the rafters on either side of the roof. The rafters on either side of the ridge beam were approximately one and a half metres, and so the interior dimensions of most houses are between 2.5 to 3 metres only. In short, the house extended in one direction since the intermediate poles propped up the beams, but the width of the house was limited by the dimensions of the rafters.

The beam–and–post prop was not an innovation since it was already used in the *ath-chala* roofs. The *ath-chala,* as the name suggests, was an eight-sided roof. This comes from the two parts of the house, a central space and the verandah, extending on all sides. The central space had a gable roof such that it sloped down in all four directions, while the verandah-like space on all four sides, also had sloping roofs. This made a total of eight slopes from which the house got its name. As discussed earlier, this house was contemporaneous to the *kumbha,* but was built by land–owning elite, who not only had access to more resources such as *murrum* and wood but were also able to hire labourers to build the house. This enabled the making of the relatively more complicated eight-sided roof. In the first part of the roof over the central space, the ridge beam is shorter than the length of the room

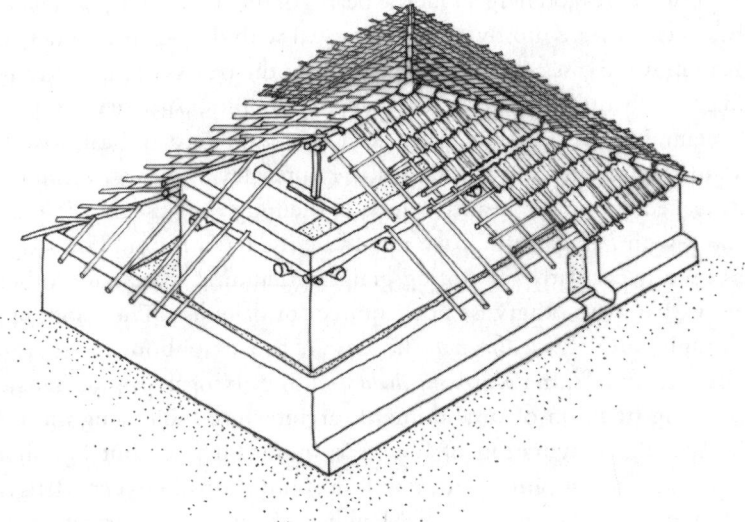

Figure 3.3 *Roof Structure of the* Ath-Chala

and thus needs intermediate supports (Figure 3.3). Two (or more, depending on the length of the room) beam-and-prop supports were placed across the width of the room and the ridge beam was supported on it. Two rafters were placed diagonally from the ends of the ridge beam to the corners of the room, which forms the profile of the four sloping sides of the roof. Other rafters were then supported between the ridge beam and the mud wall. For the second part of the roof, peg-like wooden members are inserted into the outer side of the wall of the central room. A beam is placed along the length of all four walls. Rafters are then supported between this beam and the outer mud wall. Battens are tied to both these sets of rafters after which the roofing material is added. When the mud *orak* gained currency as the commonly built type of house, the beam-and-prop detail from the *ath-chala* roof became part of the emerging *orak* structure. I discussed earlier that in terms of spatial configuration, there is little evolutionary relation between the *ath-chala* and the *orak*. The connection is, in fact, at the level of building technology and most clearly visible in the continuities in the structure of the roof.

A brief digression here about the beams of the beam–and–post detail. These beams were mostly quite substantial with diameters as much as 30 cm in some cases. They were made from the trunks of mature trees and generally quite strong. In many *ath-chala* houses, particularly where the central room was built with extra height, additional beams were provided, and a floor was added at the upper level. A layer of rafters was placed above the beams, which was enough for use as a loft, or packed with *murrum,* the space was to be used as a room. This space was used particularly for storing grain, agricultural spares, and other objects that were otherwise not required for daily use. These lofts are strikingly similar to *ath-chala* houses in the neighbouring region of Bengal. In fact, the word *ath-chala* itself is of Bengali origin. Bengal has a long tradition of rural domestic architecture built using mud.[42] The spatial configuration of houses is quite different, but building technology is the same. The political connections between Bengal and Singhbhum on account of Manbhum being an important locus of colonial governance meant that there was some regular movement of people. Particularly, the similarity of nomenclature of the *ath-chala* and the formal similarities of the lofts in the houses hint at a possible route of technology transfer between Bengal into the Singhbhum region.

In terms of detail, the same beam (of the beam–and–post detail discussed earlier) sometimes extended beyond the wall on which it was supported, i.e., it was placed such that it protruded through the mud wall to the other side (Figure 3.4). In such cases, the end of the beam was shaped into a cleft which supported a perpendicular eaves beam. The rafters were supported on the eaves beam rather than directly on the wall. In terms of roof structure, this detail, and indeed the eaves beam, was largely redundant since the mud wall was sufficient to support the rafters. What is interesting is that this detail is only found in some of the oldest houses. The age of the houses is evident from the sizes of the wooden members. Older houses tend to have large wooden beams since wood was plentiful while later houses have narrower wooden sections. So if the eaves detail was being added during the decades of transition from the *kumbha* to the *orak*, it was a vestigial practice, linked to the memory of a time when when mud walls were not in use and houses were built entirely of wood. From a

Figure 3.4 *Eaves of the Roof Supported on Beams Protruding from the Wall*

These beams are placed specifically to support the beam on which the rafters rest. This is an almost redundant detail since the beam could have rested on the wall itself.

builder's perspective, when they encounter a new material, the skills and knowledge with which they approach the process of construction are carried over from previous building experience. When people build the roof using ridge and eaves beams as the primary layer of structure, therefore, the same practice continues when building the mud *orak* as well, even though the mud walls offer new structural possibilities. It is not until families have built with mud a few times that they develop sufficient familiarity with the strength and stability it offers. Thus, it is only after a few decades that the eaves beam begins to disappear and rafters begin to be supported directly on the wall. What changed here was not just the replacement of one type of roof support with another, but the gradual supplanting of the skill and knowledge of a particular form of wooden construction with the new technological possibilities offered by mud. As long as the roof had eaves beams, it is likely that the families did not fully internalise the technological potential of mud walls. It is only when the eaves beams begin to disappear that we can definitely mark a moment of technological shift, viz., in the principles of supporting the roof on a wooden frame, to using cob walls as the primary support.

It seems self-evident that details such as the eaves beam eased out of popular memory or became redundant as new technological possibilities gained currency. However, there are a few instances of the eaves beam being put to use in recent times as well. Houses where the roof has a substantial overhang require some additional support so that it does not sag under the weight of the roofing tiles. In such cases, a series of wooden extensions are embedded in the wall, which support an eaves beam on which the rafters rest. These extensions are made of thinner wooden pieces, though the ends have notches similar to the earlier supports. In spite of the similarity in structure, the new supports present a technological shift. The difference between the two lies in the role they play within the overall structure of the roof. The former method (of internal beams extending outward to support the eaves beam) was part of the primary layer of the roof structure, while the latter is an additional prop placed to prevent the eaves end of the roof from sagging. This difference in hierarchy is underscored by the process of partial repair and reconstruction that is carried out in the houses. As and when a family acquires resources, they make amendments of the house. The roofs often get upgraded—from thatch to clay tiles or from clay tiles to roofing sheets—and the layer of wooden supports below also gets replaced. Under such circumstances, the overhang of the roof may increase compared to the earlier roof and wooden extensions are required to support the eaves. Arguably, the eaves beam as used in the *kumbha* was no longer the template for the primary structure for the roof. Instead, the eaves supports added today are similar, at least in terms of structural behaviour, to the props used elsewhere in the roof.

BETWEEN JOINERY AND MEMORY

Other parts of the roof structure were also transforming, such as the joint between the poles and ridge beam. As discussed earlier in the *kumbha,* this was made using a naturally forked branch within which the horizontal beam was placed. It was also tied for additional strength and to prevent it from moving with the force of wind or any other pressure. With the reducing access to wood over time, forked branches became scarce as well. At the same time, Adivasis were now part of agriculturalist communities, which included other types of crafts and trades people. Rulers of royal estates, influential landowners, and other leaders who formally established villages, invited ironsmiths, potters, weavers, leatherworkers and people of various castes to settle in the villages, to supply the needs of the growing village communities. Ironsmiths fashioned tools for purposes of agriculture, which indirectly led to general improvements in woodworking as well. Villagers became familiar with making ploughs, the *dhenki* (an oil press commonly found in many Adivasi houses), and wooden cots, among other things. Under such circumstances, it became possible to carve specific architectural elements out of wood as well. In place of the forked branches that were used in the *kumbha*, families began to use U-shaped pieces carved out of wood, which now formed the joint between the post and the ridge beam.

This shift appears subtle but nevertheless led to new architectural possibilities for the *orak*. The expansions of the house, previous to this development, were in the form of discrete spatial units. If a family needed an additional space they added a room alongside or perpendicular, depending on the space, to the one they already had. If the room was added alongside, the roof structure was simply extended and if the room was perpendicular, it was a separate structure with walls and a roof identical to the earlier one. Over time, perpendicular units came to be joined forming a single L-shaped house. In term of the geometry of the roof structure, this was a new challenge which did not exist in the earlier house forms. The roof now needed a hip and a valley junction which was built using the technological tool kit that Adivasis already had. The new roof conditions principally used the beam–and–post prop system though in different configurations. In one case, which represents a typical structural resolution, the L-shaped junction comprises two rooms one of which extends all the way till the edge while the other abuts the first room (Figure 3.5). In the room that extends all the way, at the point where the two ridge beams meet, a beam–and–post prop is placed to support the end of one ridge beam. The shared wall between the two spaces supports another post which props the perpendicular ridge beam. This beam extends beyond

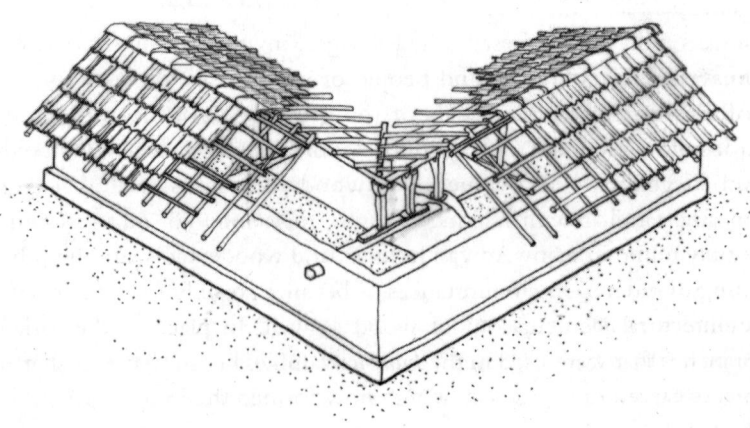

Figure 3.5 *Structure of Hip-and-Valley Junction in L-shaped Roofs*

Note the use of three props at the junction, which support the two perpendicular ridge beams.

the prop and is nailed to the first ridge beam. One rafter, the hip rafter, is placed on this joint and extends to the outer edge of the L-junction, while the rafter placed on the inner edge becomes the structure of valley rafter. The perpendicular ridge beams, and thus the L-shaped roofs become possible only because of the beam-and-post prop that was already in popular use.

Where do we locate this development within the trajectory of technological change? On the one hand, in terms of technical complexity and manner of transferring load, it is identical to how the forked branch post supported beams. Yet, in terms of making, the breaking up of the detail into a kit comprising smaller parts, viz., a beam, a post, and a U-shaped piece, gave it greater flexibility. It no longer needed to be fixed directly into the ground as with the forked branch poles and could be placed at various points along the mud wall. It was also possible to have multiple such units since it could be manufactured instead of being dependent on the forest. The greater flexibility clearly corresponds to a shift in the spatial configuration of the *orak*. Through the twentieth century, the *orak* came to comprise multiple rooms, which were enclosed around the *racha* (courtyard). Some of the largest *orak* have multiple rooms leading to complex layouts, and by extensions, complex roofs. These configurations emerge only when the beam-and-post props become commonplace. They relieve the builders of the limitations presented by the earlier processes where available lengths of wood and the forked branches determined, to a large extent, what a family could build. This is not to suggest that the developments in roof technology caused the emergence of complex configurations in domestic architecture. Yet, there is certainly a correspondence between the two developments. The social and political changes across the Singhbhum region prompted Adivasi houses to develop a more complex interiority, while building technologies simultaneously but subtly transformed alongside to produce the architectural forms we see today.

A corollary to these developments is that in spite of new spatial configurations and other changes that emerged, there were clear limits to innovation and transformation. For instance, across all the transformations of the different house types, we find only four joinery conditions (i.e., methods of joining two parts of the structure). These were:

- Tying two or more parts with a rope (as in the case of the *jhanti* and roof in the *kumbha*).
- Creating a notch in one wooden member for supporting another (as in the beam–and–post detail, ridge beam support, eaves support). The forked branch of the *kumbha* was a rudimentary form of this detail.
- Overlapping two wooden members, usually horizontal ones such as beams or rafters in a 'lap joint'. A lap joint is different from simply tying two horizontal beams because it involves cutting the ends of both the wooden members in half such that they may be placed one above the other. The lap joint is thus slightly more advanced by way of carpentry as compared to the technique of tying.
- Nailing one element with another, usually to hold them in place.

Nearly all houses built over the nineteenth and twentieth century were built using a combination of these. Tying as a method was more basic and preceded the other joinery techniques which were slightly more advanced since they required some degree of carpentry to fashion the wood into specific details. The consistent use of the same types of joints reveals that though the house itself significantly transformed over time, the joinery, using which the physical structure was built, remained largely unchanged. What we see in the instances of variations are slight changes in the dimensions of wooden members, or at most, the division of a portion of the structure into smaller constituent parts, but the basic joints remain the same. One possible explanation for this absence of innovation may be explained in terms of the frequency of building practices. Joinery in other contexts typically evolved when there were specialised guilds of woodworkers who strived to improve ways of joining wooden members and building more efficient structures. Since most Adivasis build their houses themselves and the structures can last for decades, they may undertake major construction projects only once or twice in their lifetimes. In fact, many Santal adults have never built an entire house themselves. As a result, the possibility of innovation or developing more efficient woodworking joints through repeated building gets limited.

The idea of memory came up in discussing the eaves detail of the roof where rafters continued to be supported on the eaves beam in spite of the support that the mud walls offered. The point was that even when faced with a new material, people continued to build in ways that were familiar to them from the past. A parallel case is presented by some other variations of the beam-and-post details which draw from the same technological repertoire but remain anecdotal in usage. One variation was to have three posts supporting one beam each, the ridge beam in the centre and two beams on either side. These additional beams served to support composite rafters. Usually, rafters are made of single lengths and thus limit the dimensions of interior spaces but composite rafters could be made of two pieces of wood with the joint being propped by the additional beams. This allowed the families to create a room of larger dimensions. Another variation is where families use bamboo instead of wood to make the rafters. Bamboo is naturally available in longer length and thus larger room widths are possible. Both these variations however are the exception rather than the norm. Most villagers continue to use wooden rafters of single lengths only. They buy the rafters from timber shops in small towns near the village, if they cannot procure it from the forests, but nearly never use any other material. These variations suggest that other architectural developments are possible using the same technological repertoire. So it is possible to build houses of different dimensions by applying the beam-and-post principle to the rafters in addition to the ridge beam, or by simply using a different rafter material such as bamboo. Yet, these practices did not become commonplace on account of design memory. When families decide to build a house, the pragmatics of building are intersected with an embodied sense of the form for the house. Throughout their lives they will have observed houses as being of a certain form and size, which becomes internalised as a notion of dwelling. Considering the similarities of building forms across the region, this is not restricted to individuals but is a larger shared cultural memory of the notion of dwelling.

This is seen in an example of a house where the roof was built by professional carpenters rather than the house owner herself. Here, the ridge beam is not supported by the central beam-and-post as props but by two inclined members that intersect at the top. The ridge beam then rests within the intersection. All other aspects of the structure, that is eaves, rafters and roofing material, are similar to the other roofs discussed thus far. This structure is an interesting departure from common practice because roof structures in the region typically use wooden members horizontally or vertically as discussed earlier. The use of inclined members presents two challenges. First, they require supports, i.e., some form of scaffolding during construction to hold the inclined beams in place until the mud walls are built up, dry out and attain strength. Second, inclined wooden members exert far greater force on the mud walls on account of the manner in which they are placed, and the walls need to be built strong enough to withstand this. In terms of building practice, this translates into differences in joinery, but more importantly, indicates a slightly more specialised strand of building knowledge. The woodworking requires more advanced carpentry skills and the inclined roof requires advanced planning like the mud wall requiring additional strength for supporting the roof that is yet to come. These interconnections require a comprehensive understanding of the entire structure and the detailing of each part of the structure with an awareness of the whole. In the typical *orak* on the other hand, the builder needs to focus on the part being constructed rather than conceptualise the whole structure which is an intellectually more complex task. It is not surprising then that the roof with inclined members was constructed by professional carpenters who are used to this technological complexity. What is particularly interesting is that even with the possibility of technological sophistication that the carpenters offered, the dimensions of the house remained similar to those built typically by families (Figure 3.6).

BETWEEN FAMILIARITY, INFLUENCE, SKILLS AND RESOURCES

Based on these discussions, it is apparent that Adivasi domestic architecture is produced and transformed in the interplay of resources, livelihood, skills, improvisations and memory. This provides some perspective on the limited innovation that we see. If we consider the wider socio-economic circumstances of Adivasi families, they constantly encountered new construction materials as well as new skills, processes of construction and knowledge. For instance, they

Figure 3.6 *Roof with Inclined Supports Built by professional carpenters*

encountered railway girders when working on the construction of the Bengal Nagpur line that was built across Singhbhum all the way to Calcutta.[43] Yet, there are nearly no instances of industrial construction finding their way into rural domestic architecture. There is almost no influence at the level of form as well. As such, Adivasi villagers build only houses and these are mostly of a similar size as discussed above. There are no institutional buildings, i.e., buildings apart from people's residences, to be found in the villages and no attempt to build any large-scale structures inspired by the industrial structures anywhere across the region. One possibility is that though the villagers had the exposure, there was no access to those building materials. The supply of steel and brick was restricted to the railway and factory construction sites. Considering that this was controlled by the railway authorities and the industrial houses rather than an open market, these materials did not make their way into the rural commercial networks. The village markets are known as *haat* and have historically comprised travelling salespeople and villagers who gather at fixed locations across the region to buy and trade in commodities. Even though the villagers had been familiar with industrial building materials, they would have had no access to resources to incorporate it into domestic architectural use.

This may appear to reinforce the binary that technological changes occurred in an imagined outside world while the inner world of Adivasi villages remained untouched by these changes for various reasons. In reality however, these worlds were not precise binaries that Adivasi villagers stepped in and out of. We will never be able to enter the Adivasi villagers' minds to identify what they experienced when they worked on the construction site and then returned to their own *kumbha* or *orak*. What we do know is that industrial processes were becoming part of Adivasi life with new forms of livelihood, wages, and new systems of labour. These had an indirect impact on technologies of house building, where families could buy materials by paying for it in cash. This, arguably, set the stage for the commodification of both resources and labour, within domestic construction. That the skilled labourers had limited impact on significantly transforming the architecture of the *orak* is linked to the perception of dwelling itself and the extent to which that changed over time. This should also be viewed against the wider material cultural trait of sparseness. Compared to many cultures where the house is a site of significant resource investment because it is an anchor for individual status and identity, this is not the case among Santals and other Adivasis. The transformation of building technology without the widespread incorporation of unambiguously modern materials such as brick, steel, and concrete problematises both architectural and Adivasi modernity. Modern architecture, in popular imagination though not necessarily in critical discourses, is associated with such building materials and technologies. Adivasis were familiar with the technologies but did not always have the opportunity and conditions that enabled their use. Architectural modernity begins to appear as a fragmentary trope, or rather, a meshwork of multiple kinds of knowledge, skills, structures of resource access, individual volition and collective memory, each of which are in turn intersected by multiple influences to produce decisive breaks from the past.

Chapter 4

The Transformation of Domestic Art

Visiting Adivasi villages across the Singhbhum region over the years offers convincing evidence that the murals or even simple wall paintings done by Santal families are distinctive from those of other communities. In the previous chapter I discussed various points of continuity between the social, economic, historical and architectural aspects of Santals and other Adivasi and rural non-Adivasi communities. In fact, in the discussion on technology, it is developed as a category of knowledge and practice common across the rural areas of Singhbhum and maybe even south Jharkhand more broadly, irrespective of caste and ethnicity. In the case of domestic art, however, the dividing lines are more sharply drawn. It is a common refrain among the villagers that nobody paints and decorates their houses like the Santal *manjhi*. When interactivity in so many spheres of Adivasi life has and continues to produce similar spatial practices, it is intriguing to find a distinctive tradition of Santal art. The walls of the houses are painted after the monsoons, usually in the months of October or November in Singhbhum. The heavy rains dull the appearance of the walls. Also, this is the time when the paddy crop is nearly ready to be harvested and harvest festivals such as the Santal Sohrai are celebrated. From a phenomenological perspective, the act of painting the wall is not mere decoration. Viewed through the lens of Eliade's classic text on symbolic making of place, the periodic acts of plastering and painting are akin to a process of renewal of a place. They eliminate impurities and dirt and symbolically speaking, become re-enactments of a 'primordial transformation of chaos into cosmos by the divine act of creation'.[44] The house is seen as sullied by use in the previous state, and the process of plastering and painting becomes the purifying gesture. Most communities that build using earth, the world over, have annual processes of repair and painting, which are typically combined with a festive event and carry great symbolic import of this kind. The specifics of design or practice notwithstanding, domestic art is clearly an important dimension of the architecture and therefore of the act of dwelling itself.

CYCLES OF PLASTERING AND PAINTING

There are a number of plastering, painting and decorative practices carried out by Adivasi women. They apply some plaster at the threshold of the doors of the house every day as a ritual practice, plaster the floors of the entire house twice or three times a week and paint murals on the walls every year. Floor plastering is a particularly symbolic act. The first task for women as soon as they wake up every morning is to apply circular patches of cow dung at the entrances to the house and various spaces within the house. Mud stoves that are used for cooking in Santal dwellings are similarly believed to go 'stale' and require plastering before use each time (Figure 4.1). In addition to these daily rituals, the entire house and the part of the *kulhi* in front of the house is plastered twice or three times a week. Floor plastering is important for two reasons—first, for functional reasons, since the dwellings are made of mud, the floors require frequent reworking to maintain the surface. Second, for ritual reasons, because the house is believed to get impure with daily use. The term used by Santali women was *basi*, which translates as stale. Plastering the house, particularly with cow dung, purifies the premises and makes it suitable for habitation once again.

The plastering of the house typically begins in the morning after the cattle have left for grazing. Women begin with the part of the *kulhi* in front of their house. Small lumps of dried cow dung are mixed with water by hand and poured onto the *kulhi* surface. This mixture is spread around with a broom to cover the required surface area while ensuring that no puddles of water remain (Figure 4.2). The women take particular care that the edges of the plastered surface are precise and neat.

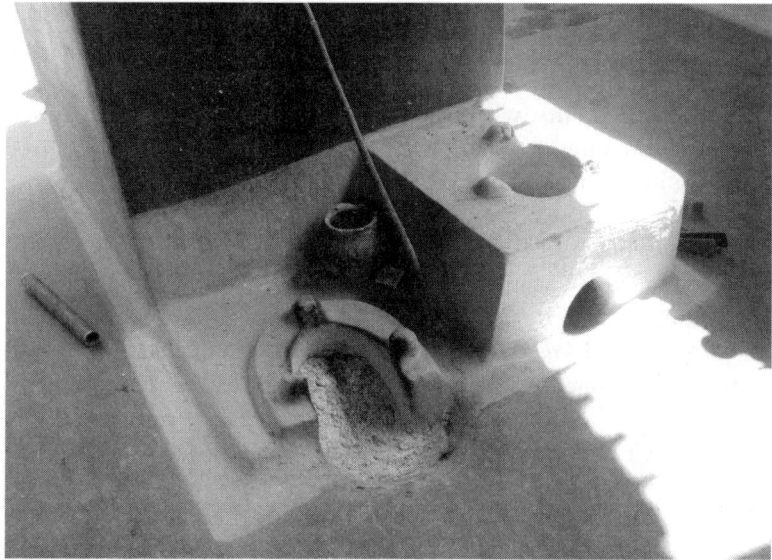

Figure 4.1 *Mud-Plastered Chula*

Figure 4.2 *Plastering the* kulhi *in Front of the House*

The extent of this plastered surface usually corresponds to the width of the house but there are subtle differences across villages. In Bhagabondhi, women plaster half the width of the *kulhi* in front of their houses such that when the task is completed, the entire street is covered with a fresh coat of plaster. In Haudah, the *kulhi* has a tarred surface which is nearly 30 cm higher than the mud surfaces on either side. Here, women plastered the mud surfaces near the entrance to their houses but extend the plastering up to the edge of the tarred road and cover a narrow strip on the tarred surface as well. It almost appears as a gesture of plastering the *kulhi* without actually doing so. Bandudih also has a tarred *kulhi* and a large volume of vehicular traffic such as trucks and tractors carrying quarried stone through the village. Here, women only plaster the patch of ground immediately in front of their own house, rather than covering half the *kulhi* as in the case of Bhagabondhi.

In any case, irrespective of the extent of plastering or the surface of the *kulhi*, regular plastering of the floor is an important daily activity. It is also a very time-consuming and laborious task. The women explained that doing this was important for the house to appear neat and tidy. One woman pointed out that Santals do not bother much with their personal appearance but take considerable care to keep their houses well maintained. Since they described the plastering as *achchha* (good) or *saaf-suthra* (clean and neat) rather than *sundar* (beautiful), it is evident that the practices of plastering and painting serve larger purposes in the maintenance of buildings and are not merely ornamental or decorative. The plastering of the *kulhi* suggests that this is also a participative activity in the village community through collective upkeep of the built environment of the village. This is seen in Bhagabondhi where the entire *kulhi* gets resurfaced through the contributions of individual houses. As a corollary, a sense of community solidarity may also be gauged through the level of maintenance of the dwellings and the *kulhi*. In villages facing any form of crisis, major or minor, the *kulhi* and to some extent the houses tend to be poorly kept. This became strikingly visible in the village of Phulgoda which I visited during a preliminary research phase. Phulgoda was an economically stressed village since the crops had failed two years in a row due to poor rainfall. There was also conflict over leadership positions within the village community. While this is probably not the only reason for the lack of maintenance of the *kulhi*, it is a distinct possibility, because if a village community is internally conflicted, the inclination to collectively maintain the *kulhi* or to labour over painting the front wall of the house may not remain a priority for families.

The interior spaces of the houses are also plastered along with the *kulhi*. There is a key difference in technique between the plastering of the interior and exterior spaces. Compared to the *kulhi* which is washed with a thin cow dung mixture using a broom, the interior spaces are plastered with a piece of cloth dipped in a mixture of cow dung, ash and water, sometimes even some colour, and applied over all the floor surfaces. Cow dung is used for the courtyard, while other materials such as ash and colours, usually a shade of maroon, is used for the interiors of individual spaces. The technique of plastering is noteworthy: women apply horizontal strokes with their hand resulting in nearly square patches of plaster that cover the entire floor surface. They take particular care to ensure that the strokes are even and that the edges of the plastered surface are sharply defined (Figure 4.3). While women from other communities do occasionally plaster the floors of their houses, it is only Santal women who perform this task with such frequency and care. The performance and the resulting plastered surfaces are distinctive on two counts—first, when compared with many other mud-plastering practices the world over, one finds that the natural

Figure 4.3 *Courtyard Floor Covered in Horizontal Strokes*

gesture of the hand appears to produce an arc rather than straight lines. Stephen Huyler's photographic documentation of women's domestic art practices identifies a number of examples where the texture of the painted surface clearly suggests the particular bodily gestures, more specifically hand movements that produced strokes of a certain kind.[45] That Santal women in Singhbhum work with straight strokes, appears counter-intuitive to a more natural movement and thus intentionally aimed at producing a particular kind of aesthetic effect. Also, this technique is similar to the manner in which the murals are painted, a point to which I will return in the next section of this chapter.

In term of materials, cow dung is preferred for the plastering of floors since it is considered that it purifies the surfaces on which it is applied. However, the use of cow dung as a plastering material competes with its other uses, as fuel for instance. This equation becomes important given that cow dung is often scarce and its availability hinges upon a number of factors. To begin with, cow dung is collected from the animal shelters within a dwelling after the cows have been taken away for grazing in the morning. Women clean out the shelters by collecting any dung that may have been deposited in the night. Many families today, however, have small herds of cattle or no cattle at all depending on the nature of agricultural activities within a family. This is usually a result of repeated divisions of land on account of inheritance over generations, or also common in cases where families primarily draw their livelihood from wage labour. Such families may not be significantly involved in agricultural activities any more. In the absence of their own herds of cattle, women or young girls follow other grazing herds in order to collect dung. When faced with such scarcity, the cow dung is reserved for ritual plastering of the house or for other particularly auspicious days, such as Thursdays, while *murrum* is used for the routine plastering of the floor. What further stresses the availability of cow dung is that it gets used as fuel for cooking, when other fuels such as wood or *gundi* (dried lumps made of mud and coal dust) are not available. Shifts in resource availability bring out some important features of the floor-plastering practice, which is that the practice remains important, but the materials used vary according to available resources. The change in material also embeds a shift in the meaning of the practices, since the purifying role is now played by the act of plastering rather than by the use of cow dung.

Figure 4.4 *Santal Houses in Herang*

Figure 4.5 *Internal Walls Painted to Distinguish Territories of Different Family Units*

Figure 4.6 *Floral Motifs in Seraikela Appreciated by Villagers*

Figure 4.7 *Geometric Motifs in Seraikela Murals*

Figure 4.8 *Sculpted Columns in a Santal House in Seraikela*

Figure 4.9 *Elaborately Painted Mural from Purulia, A Region That Earlier Witnessed Disturbance but Is Now Relatively Peaceful*

Figure 4.10 *Santal Mural from Hazaribagh. Note the Muted Colour Palette*

Figure 4.11 *Kurmi Mural with Animal Motifs Using a Stencil Technique*

MURALS: MAKING AND SIGNIFICANCE

Mural painting takes place towards the end of the calendar year. By this time the monsoon rains have stopped and the paddy, depending on the region and variety of paddy planted, may be ready or almost ready for harvest. Women begin preparing for the task of painting murals from September or early October. As such, the process of constructing the walls ensures that they are largely protected from the rain. The walls are typically built quite thick, ranging from 35 to 45 cm, which ensures that the structure is not affected by water erosion. The smooth plastering and painting further create a surface that allows rain to wash off the wall surface immediately. The roof of the house also overhangs considerably and protects most of the wall from rain. The process of plastering and preparing the wall for paint begins after the wall is built and the roofs are added. This task is carried out almost entirely by women, who are responsible for finishing the house from this point onwards. The plaster is made of very fine *murrum mati*, mixed with cow dung and bits of straw or rice husk. This *murrum* is finer than that used for the construction of the walls and is usually collected from pond beds or beds of other water bodies in the vicinity of the village. The straw or husk serves to reinforce the plaster layer and prevents it from cracking. Women apply the plaster mixture on the wall by hand and smoothen it out to as flat a surface as possible. When it has set, but is still a little damp, women scrub the surface with a stone, to make it very smooth. After this surface dries, a thin layer of cow dung is applied as a wash on the wall, after which it is ready to be painted.

There is a clear hierarchy in the manner and sequence in which the surfaces are painted. Only the exterior walls of the dwelling are painted in colours, while the interiors of rooms are usually just painted white. Even within the exterior walls, women pay particular attention to the front elevation that faces the street. This is the first wall to be painted to ensure that they do not run short of colours. Other walls may be painted with diluted colours or even left plain if they run short. On the outer walls, particularly those facing the *kulhi,* the overall design scheme broadly comprises horizontal bands of colour with a dark base in the form of a *pide* (plinth used as seat at the base of the wall) and other colours above (Figure 4.4). The colours typically used are white, ochre, red, black (from burnt straw or rubber tyres these days) and blue (from mixing chemical indigo with white clay). These colours are naturally occurring clays or oxides found in the Singhbhum region, but are not necessarily available near every village. Villagers travel considerable distances to procure the necessary colours for their walls.

The painting of the wall is not just an act of decoration but becomes an important marker of a family's property. This is evident particularly in cases where extended families occupied a single dwelling. The family units living together may include a nuclear family living together with elderly parents, unmarried or widowed siblings or two or three nuclear families (such as two or three brothers and their wives and children). The different family units will use some spaces as shared ones, while some spaces are used exclusively by each family unit. In Bhagabondi, for instance, an elderly widowed lady lived with her two unmarried daughters, one unmarried son, and widowed daughter-in-law and her daughter (the elderly lady's granddaughter). Their house had three different cooking and sleeping areas, *tulsi pinda* (a small mud platform with the sacred *tulsi* plant growing on it) and mud stoves in the court-yard for parboiling paddy. Each of these was used exclusively by the elderly lady, the daughter-in-law or the two unmarried daughters respectively. The unmarried son had a separate sleeping area but no cooking or worship areas since he ate food with his mother. The spatial differentiation between the family units was underscored by the paint-ings on the inner walls of the house (Figure 4.5). The front wall was painted as a single surface, but the walls facing the courtyard were painted in different colours indicating the territories of the different family units. So, externally this was a single house, while internally, the family units differentiated their individual territories using murals. In some cases, especially when adjacent houses share a common front wall, each family paints the part of the front wall that belongs to them, and so even the external walls indicate differences in ownership.

Across Singhbhum, mural designs are broadly of two types, the first scheme with broad horizontal bands of colour, which may be consid-ered a generic design scheme used by Adivasi and rural non-Adivasi communities across the region. The second scheme also principally has horizontal bands but with geometric or floral motifs added within it. In either case, the process of painting begins with marking the design on the wall. Women hold a tight rope across the wall and mark the horizontal bands. Colours are prepared by mixing the previously pro-cured clays with water. A piece of cloth is dipped in the mixture and rubbed on the wall. Women work with very precise horizontal strokes to create blocks of colour at a time and they move across the wall by painting vertical columns of colour. The performance of painting and the resultant effect is very similar to the way in which women plaster the floors of the interior parts of their house. For the interior floors, women use a piece of cloth dipped in a dung or ash mixture, while exterior ground surfaces such as those of the open yards are covered with a thin layer of cow dung plaster applied using a broom. As with the wall, they work in blocks until the entire floor surface is covered. In both cases, women pay particular attention to using horizontal strokes, producing a smooth and even surface, and ensuring precise edges for the plastered and painted surfaces.

The similarities between the floor plastering and wall painting tech-niques, hints at the continuity between the two practices. In the previous chapter, I discussed that the graduation to mud construction was rooted in a familiarity with working with *murrum*. This was partly through agriculture, where Adivasis cleared land to make it cultivable, but partly also in the use of mud for plastering the floor of the *kumbha*. The first signs of consolidation of the *kumbha* occurred when families began to plaster the *jhanti* walls. During this time, the technique and performance of plaster must have carried over from the floors to the walls. Where this continuity becomes even more important is in the nature of design schemes that emerge on walls. The dominant design scheme is of horizontal bands, irrespective of other details that may be added within this. Considering the bodily gesture through which these designs are produced, the horizontality of the design and the aesthetics of precision are rooted in the performance of wall painting itself.

Also interesting is the precision with which the work is carried out. On both the floors and the walls, Santal women pride themselves on producing surfaces covered with neat strokes and precise edges. In conversation, they simply said it was good (*accha lagta hai*) or that it looks neat (*saaf lagta hai*). But there is, in fact, a much more widespread

cultural acceptance and indeed expectation of doing very precise plastering and painting. When I had almost completed fieldwork in the
first village during my doctoral research, I organised an exhibition of
the architectural documentation I had carried out. I had hoped to find
out more about how the villagers perceived their built environment
and my documentation of it. In one village, a significant part of the
display comprised photographs of murals, since this particular village
had a number of large and spectacularly painted murals. The audience,
both men and women from the village, were unanimous on their
choice of one mural which had pink and green diagonal lines and a
flower-like geometric motif on a white background (Figure 4.6). They
explained that the design was good since it did not have crooked lines,
not too many colours had been used, and that the design resembled
blooming flowers. In another instance, watching me photograph a
particular wall, my guide pointed out that the wall was not particularly
well painted since the edges of the blocks of colour were not precise.
They slightly overlapped each other to create a fuzzy edge. While we
cannot surmise that these comments represent a universal Santal aesthetic, it does indicate that precision is an important concern for Santal
women artists.

TRIGGERS FOR DESIGN DEVELOPMENT

The mural discussed above was painted in a village in the Seraikela
region of Singhbhum. Villages across Seraikela tend to have more
complex designs than those in other regions. They often include large
and complex geometric shapes or floral motifs within the basic design
scheme of horizontal bands of colour (Figures 4.7 and 4.8). The differences in design are to some extent linked to the technique by which
the murals are produced. I discussed earlier that the horizontal bands
are painted in horizontal strokes with a piece of cloth. The elaborate
design schemes differ from the horizontal band schemes in three ways.
First, they cannot be executed with cloth dipped in colour but require
the use of a brush. In some cases the bands of colour that form that
background for geometric patterns or motifs are painted with cloth
while the details are added with a brush, while in other cases, the entire
wall is painted using a brush. Second, the palette of colours observed

here is much wider and indeed brighter since villagers in this region use artificial colours more than what was observed in other case study villages. Third, in terms of time, elaborate patterns take much longer to execute as compared to a wall with bands of colour, which can be completed in two or three hours. Consequently, the development of elaborate designs is not just a shift in forms but in the associated resources and knowledge as well. The question that emerges is how and why did such a shift occur in Seraikela alone, as compared to other parts of the Singhbhum region. Before moving to that discussion, it is important to iterate that there is a similarity of wall-painting tradition across the entire region but that the trajectory of design development diverged in Seraikela. This was evident in cases where an already painted wall became damaged due to untimely rains or when women ran short of time for painting on account of other domestic responsibilities. In such cases, they painted the walls in plain bands of colour as a temporary measure until they found time to add details or until the next cycle of painting. It becomes clear that even with transformations in design, the horizontal ordering of the design scheme remains important.

A key difference in the Seraikela murals is the use of paint brushes. This presents both a technical and a conceptual shift from the perspective of the women artists. First, it is technical in that it brings about a number of material changes such as in the consistency of colours used. It also changes the bodily gesture of painting itself, since brushes are typically used in vertical rather than horizontal strokes. Second, it is a conceptual shift given that earlier memories of painting, both in terms of performance and design, must now be negotiated in terms of the possibilities afforded by the new medium of the brush. So even with a brush, women continue to paint horizontal bands, but the bands are now wider in order to be painted in vertical strokes. In the previous chapter, I discuss how technological possibilities intersect with memories of dwelling to inform the ways in which people build. Often, in spite of new possibilities, villagers continue to use materials or produce forms that they are familiar with. The same seems to happen in the case of the murals. Women paint using horizontal strokes but in phases of vertical blocks, resulting in long horizontal bands of colour. Even though the brush is used in vertical strokes, they do not shift to painting in vertical bands. Bodily performance is meshed with a particular form and aesthetic, which persists even when a new bodily performance replaces the older one.

It is important to elucidate the conditions under which the use of brushes became commonplace in the Seraikela region. Given the otherwise sparse material culture of Santal communities and the primarily paddy cultivating way of life, the brush does not naturally feature in Santal daily life. Santal families typically own tools such as knives, axes and spades, agricultural implements such as carts, fishing equipment, and domestic items such as utensils. Using a brush is not a skill embedded in the practices of everyday lives of typical Santal families and was obviously acquired by Santal women somewhere beyond the village. One possible site is the many construction sites and small-scale industrial establishments that dot the landscape of Seraikela. While Singhbhum in general has a high concentration of industrial and mining activity, Seraikela particularly has large numbers of small- and medium-scale manufacturing industries where Santals and other Adivasis are employed as labourers. Two factors underlie this equation of Adivasi involvement as construction and industrial labourers in this part of Singhbhum. First, compared to other parts of Singhbhum such as the river valleys of the Subernarakha and Kharkai Rivers, the Seraikela region is less fertile and has lower agricultural productivity. Therefore, more Adivasi families seek employment as wage labourers in order to earn their livelihood. Second, the nature of wage employment is different in Seraikela. Compared to other areas where industrial activities are in the form of mining or heavy metallurgical industries, Seraikela is developing as a small-scale industrial belt and has therefore seen significant construction activity. It is this form of wage labour that most likely created the possibility of exposure to the use of brushes, which then became a part of the Santal domestic art repertoire. It is the particular economic and geographic conditions of Sereikela that led to the use of brushes, on account of which new wall-painting possibilities emerged.

The exposure to brushes however is not sufficient impetus for their use. The women artists require appropriate paints as well. As the use of brushes and artificial paints became probable and popular, they must have become more easily available. Domestic needs and everyday goods used by villagers are typically made at home, as in the case of brooms or fishing traps, or purchased at weekly markets, as in the case of clothes and cosmetics. In Haudah, for instance, Delabira is the nearest weekly market where travelling salesmen set up stalls selling clothes, vegetables, cosmetics, medicines, tools and household essentials. Such markets are held at various locations on different days of the week and villagers usually visit the market nearest to them. Many salesmen at these markets were Adivasi villagers and earned their living by buying goods from Jamshedpur (the nearest urban centre) and selling them across the region. The high mobility of the salesmen allows them to gauge people's requirements quite well. When brushes and paints began to become popular, therefore, they came to be supplied in the markets more regularly as well.

MOBILITY AND INSPIRATION

The wide range of designs observed across the Seraikela include bold geometric patterns, floral motifs, and in one example, elaborate sculpted columns as well. What is interesting, is that particular designs are local-ised within villages, rather than being similar or common across the region. In order to understand the localisation of the motifs, one needs to examine the sources of design inspiration and therefore examine women's mobility, since it is they who conceptualise and execute these works. On asking where women drew their inspiration from, they often answered that they drew whatever they liked. While it is beyond the scope of this study to suggest how particular visual forms emerge in Santal wall paintings or what their relationship to women's everyday experiences of their environments may be, one may safely contend that women draw inspiration from each other, given that designs within a village appear similar over time and that women spend most of their time in the village itself. In other words, one cannot conjecture how design innovation occurs in the first instance, but having occurred, it does disseminate within the village on account of women's internal movements. Even neighbouring villages may not influence each other because women have no occasion to interact with other villages, except their maternal homes. During fieldwork, I observed that women often did not appear to know about houses at the end of their *kulhi*. They questioned me about other houses I visited, and when I asked why they did not know, they said that they had no reason to visit other houses far from their own. Women did however walk into their immediate neighbours' houses and go as far as the nearest well or hand pump to fetch water. In short, women's movements within the village are restricted to the vicinity of their own homes or the nearest source of water and consequently, design developments are similar within and largely limited to the vicinity of individual villages alone.

The relationship between women's mobility and design development also raises questions about the temporality of the development. So, while women draw inspiration from other women, it must be remembered that wall painting is an individual act rather than a collective one. Over what period of time do designs spread and become popular in a village? Considering the process of painting and women's mobility in greater detail provides some clues? During a single season of painting (typically in October or November) women begin painting their walls, while simultaneously managing their other domestic and agricultural responsibilities. Given that the walls have to be ready before Sohrae, which is the main harvest festival for Santals, the window for completing the painting task is quite small. Additionally, prior to the actual painting, women plan the designs and procure necessary material such as colours. All this has to be done in tandem with the domestic and agricultural chores that women perform. So even if women saw interesting designs being executed by other women, they are unlikely to be able to modify their own plans and paint the new design immediately. They would typically wait until the following year before they can introduce any new designs or elements in their walls. This means that design ideas will require at least two or three annual cycles of painting before they become popular and common in a village.

The possibility of a slow spread of design ideas is exemplified in the case of Mahotabeda, which has unique sculpted columns in many houses in the village. To make these, columns are first built in square or rectangular forms and are then carved into the desired shapes and painted. In subsequent years, columns may be repainted but not carved again since that would make the columns weak. In terms of popular building practice, these columns are both unusual, elaborate, and time consuming to construct. So if one or two families in Mahotabeda decided, at some point in the past, to introduce an element such as a sculpted column, and other families wished to adopt the idea, they must have waited until the next cycle of building and painting in order to incorporate it into their own dwellings. In this manner, over a few annual cycles of painting, a complex design idea may spread within a village.

Having framed the transformation in wall-painting designs within memories of past practices and possibilities afforded by new media, i.e., paint brushes, it is important to ask why Seraikela alone became the site of such developments. A brief history of the nature of political rule in Seraikela offers some clues. Compared to Dalbhum and other parts of East Singhbhum that were under colonial governments prior to Indian independence, Seraikela was a royal estate. It is a well-known fact that the royal family was considered repressive. One example of repression was the implementation of a form of tax which decreed that if any subject of Seraikela possessed anything that was better than the ruler's own possessions, the ruler was entitled to claim it as his own. This was known as the Nazrana Tax.[46] Elderly villagers recollect that no one was allowed to build or decorate their dwellings better than the ruler's own palace. With the merger of royal estates and the Indian Union after Independence in 1947, Santals were no longer compelled to paint their houses in a simple fashion and this was a possible trigger for elaborate design developments in the region. It corresponds to elderly villagers' observation that the elaborate designs seen on walls today are a recent development and were unheard of two or three generations ago. In other words, in the decades since the dissolution of the royal rule in Seraikela, around Indian independence, Santals began to develop more elaborate wall-painting designs. Seen against the background of the political climate of Seraikela, the profusion of elaborate designs may have emerged as a reaction to a history of aesthetic repression in the region. This historical factor considered together with the close correlation between women's restricted mobility and the development of wall painting designs and practices as taking place primarily within villages themselves may also serve to explain why these practices did not extend beyond the Seraikela region as a whole.

GEOGRAPHIES OF INTERACTIVITY, IDENTITY, AND DESIGN

If we were to sketch a broad geography of mural designs, then the south Jharkhand region does have somewhat distinct motifs and practices in particular localities. The Seraikela region in the north Singhbhum produces elaborate murals with motifs, while the south, east and west have murals in the form of bands. Further north towards Hazaribagh, we encounter a very different palette of colours and a wide range of mural traditions produced by communities other than Santals. Across the region, however, countering any idea of a regional coherence or similarity of practice, are the localised developments which depend on the women artists' mobility and exposure, but also on wider contextual conditions such as economic prosperity and socio-political stability. In the Ranchi district, which lies immediately north of Singhbhum, are a number of Adivasi villages including ones with Santal families. Ranchi and Singhbhum are separated by the Dalma Hill Range. The hill areas and the villages to the north witnessed much violence in the 1990s and 2000s on account of Naxalite movements, which have abated to some extent in the past decade.[47] One village that I visited in 2014 had some exceptionally elaborate murals (Figure 4.9). The houses were old and large providing a vast canvas. Five murals in the village were particularly remarkable, covered with detailed motifs of flowers, insects, and butterflies. Further, each wall had different kinds of motifs using multiple colours. They had used brushes to paint the minute details with great care and the entire effort had clearly taken the women a lot of time. What was interesting was that these houses stood out even within the village where other houses were painted with simple bands. Apart from the question of inspiration, which arguably came from popular visual culture, these women artists clearly had the time to paint such murals over a period of four or five weeks. They were able to hire agricultural labourers to work in their fields, which freed up some time for the women to paint. Also, the fact that the details, even in the form of smalls motifs, had not yet appeared on any other village house suggested that it was a relatively recent development. It is likely that with the recent abatement of tensions across the region, women artists have once again begun to pay attention to mural decoration. In consonance with the earlier discussion about murals and inter-community relationships, their production and the fact that they are flourishing are an approximate index of the general well-being of Adivasi communities.

The Hazaribagh region, further north of Ranchi, presents an interesting contrast to Singhbhum. Here, Santal murals have very different designs and a muted palette. Hazaribagh Santal women artists paint on an ochre background with the lower half of the wall containing geometric motifs such as diagonal or orthogonal stripes. These are painted using a combination of red, black, or white (Figure 4.10). Occasionally, women paint flowers in a series such that it visually appears as a horizontal band. Apart from the horizontality, however, the Hazaribagh murals have neither the precision nor the bright artificial colours typical in Singhbhum. What is intriguing, however, is that other communities such as Kurmi, Agaria, Ganju, and Oraon have vastly different mural practices. Ganju women draw animals such as cows, snakes, deer which are native to the region. Oraon women artists paint flowers, while Agaria women paint floral and animal motifs (Figure 4.11). Kurmi murals, for instance, are made using a profusion of dots and lines to create abstract motifs representing Pashupati (the lord of animals) and his consort. The techniques of painting are also varied. The dominant technique is painting but this is done both in the form of applying different colours in the background and foreground to produce the patterns and using a stencil technique where darker colours are applied such that the light background is left exposed thus creating the desired design. A more complex technique used only by Kurmi women artists is comb-cutting (Figure 4.12).[48] Women apply dark clay in the background followed by a layer of paler clay which is almost white in colour. When this layer is just set but not fully dry, it is scraped off with a comb or some other toothed instrument revealing the dark lines from the surface below. This technique produces a delicately hued mural. The Kurmi women paint animal motifs such as tigers, peacocks, deer, and flowers and decorative borders. Today, many of these mural practices are limited to a few villages, where they continue only with the constant encouragement offered by a local organisation.

Figure 4.12 *Kurmi Mural with Animal Motifs Done Using the Comb-cutting Technique*

What is significant in Hazaribagh is the distinctiveness of the mural designs and painting practices along community lines. Though these communities live close to each other and the women artists must have at least a nominal knowledge of the different mural practices, their own designs remained distinctly different. This seems counter to the earlier discussion about women drawing inspiration from each other's designs, but what we witness in Hazaribagh is not a circulation of ideas in the realm of the everyday, but a larger, almost public articulation of the relationship between social identity and mural art. The past few decades have seen rising social and political consciousness about being Adivasi in Jharkhand and, at least in the case of Hazaribagh, mural art has emerged as its concomitant. The walls of public institutions in cities such as Hazaribagh, Ranchi, and Jamshedpur, are decorated with mural art drawn from these rural traditions. They are known as Khovar or Sohrai art, which refers to the art practices of certain communities. In due course, in popular discourses proliferated by the State and other cultural institutions, these mural traditions have become synonymous with certain Adivasi or non-Adivasi groups. While it is difficult to speculate about the impact that these developments have had on women's own sources of inspiration and design ideas, we do see the emergence of the idea of distinctive mural traditions, which supercede, or indeed even notionally erase the diversity of designs and practices that we see in everyday life.

The relationship between domestic art practices and identity is much more fluid in everyday life than the popular imagination around mural art would suggest. One site where this clearly plays out is in the making of *alpana* or decorative and ritual floor designs in villages where Santals, other Adivasi, and non-Adivasi communities reside together. As such, *alpana* is known as a Hindu practice rather than an Adivasi one. Santals, however, have many different ideas about *alpana*. In villages where Santal families make *alpana* designs, it is accepted as part of the Santal domestic art repertoire, while in others, Santals distinguish it as a Hindu practice. During fieldwork, I observed the practice of making *alpana* in Bhagabondhi and Bondudih. Santals lived together with Mahato, Munda, and Gop families in these villages, all of whom made *alpana* on a weekly basis. Santals lived with Mahato families in Bhagabondhi, though in separate neighbourhoods. Some families were making *alpana* designs at their front doors on Thursday, which was considered auspicious across the village. In Bondudih, Santal families lived in a mixed neighbourhood with Munda and Gop families and did not make *alpana*. They clearly stated that they did not do so because it was a Hindu practice. In Haudah, where only Santal families lived, there were no instances of *alpana*. Irrespective of how we position *alpana* vis-à-vis social identity, the difference raises some interesting issues about the appropriation of non-Adivasi practices among Adivasis such as Santals and the contexts in which these occur. As I mentioned earlier, in Bondudih, *alpana* is not practised because of its identification by Santals as a distinctly Hindu practice and Santal families have not adopted it. Munda women in the village too pointed out that only Hindus made *alpana* designs, while Adivasi families did not. In this case, they were referring to Santals as Adivasis. They further added that they, i.e., Mundas, were also Adivasi but they still made *alpana*. Mundas are largely considered to be more Hinduised in comparison to other Adivasi communities. What emerges here is fluidity, not just in the association of art, but of intra-village identities as well, because even when using the term Adivasi to describe both themselves and Santals, Munda women implied a distinction between the two.

In Bhagabondhi, the making of *alpana* by only a few Santal families opens up other dimensions of identity. Three Santal families regularly made *alpana*. Two of these families were of the *manjhi* (headman) and the elected ward member of the village respectively, while the third was a young girl who enjoyed drawing *alpana*. Compared to the *manjhi*, who is the social head of the village community and holds a hereditary position, the ward member is an elected member of the ward (administrative unit comprising a few villages) within which the village is located. Both positions were considered important in Bhagabondhi and both men were considered community leaders with considerable social standing. Women from these families said that they drew the *alpana* because it looked beautiful. They drew it as the finishing touches to the front door after plastering the floors. This motivation to make *alpana* is interesting on two counts. First, it is made primarily for its aesthetic considerations though the ritual significance may have been adopted, given that the motifs of Goddess Lakshmi's feet are drawn for auspiciousness, and second, that not all Adivasi houses along the *kulhi* chose to do it. Only the families of men who were in leadership positions in the village had adopted the practices and this may be the reason for women to have the license to do so without drawing censure from the wider community. When comparing these two cases, it is apparent that in Bondudih, the absence of *alpana* becomes a register of Adivasi identity in the midst of Hindu neighbours, while in Bhagabondhi *alpana* was an assertion of a privileged position within the community.

Chapter 5

Of *Kulhi* and Community

As Adivasi houses transformed, so did the larger spatial and social fabric that the houses were a part of. Sedentarisation led to an increase in settled villages across the region. Due to the policies of land allocation for revenue collection, the villages became spatially fixed and bounded. In the process, the relationships between individual Adivasi families, the community, and the land and forests in the vicinity became codified in very specific ways. Adivasi institutions such as the *kulhi* and the *jahira* became fixed within the landscape of Adivasi inhabitation, possibly for the first time. The *kulhi* is the central street and the *jahira* is the sacred grove for Santal collective worship, though other communities have similar groves. Both these sites have a number of symbolic practices and taboos associated with them, which are fundamental to the spiritual well-being of the communities associated with them. Prior to the mid-nineteenth century, when communities migrated across Chotanagpur and beyond, both these sites were, at best, temporary spatial agreements. The *kulhi* emerged in the arguably liminal street spaces that connected the *kumbha* of the different families of the band travelling together. The *jahira* too was temporarily ascribed to a specific location that was identified by the group. When the group moved on, a new *kulhi* and *jahira* were established. With the formation of revenue villages, both these institutions consolidated, but more importantly, also became sites where the idea of community was spatially negotiated.

The idea of the *kulhi*, which is otherwise basically a street, as an institution is interesting considering that the space of the *kulhi* is visually vague. In both formation and use, it emerges rather than being formally defined. Yet, it is socially potent, as evidenced by narratives of rituals and practices embedded in the place. Bodding, who produced a seminal work on Santal society, refers extensively to social institutions such as the *akhara* which was a part of the *kulhi* where ceremonial dances were held. This was also the place where the *kulhi durup* or the village council met. It is these practices taking place in the *kulhi* that lend the place the stature of an institution. This idea resonates with other indigenous societies where the landscape of inhabitation is imbued with value through memories and practices of everyday living rather than being presented as visual images. The visual vagueness was further compounded by the fact that the idea of community itself was a multivalent one. It depended, as I discuss later in this chapter, on the context and specificities of interaction between different villagers (for instance, whether they were men, women or younger people) and myself. This chapter explores the points of correspondence between the morphology of the Adivasi village neighbourhood and various everyday practices, to identify how notions of community are spatially enforced and negotiated, both in the past and present moments.

MORPHOLOGY OF THE *KULHI*

Santal villages are typically linear in layout with houses located on either side of the *kulhi*. Linear geometry is a distinct characteristic of Santal settlements since other Adivasi and non-Adivasi rural communities in the region tend to have clustered layouts, which is a branching network rather than a single central street. In some cases, there is a central *kulhi* but it forks into two and two or more *kulhi* may intersect each other at various points within the village. In Santal settlements, however, the linearity of the *kulhi* is strictly adhered to and we rarely find any branching or intersecting streets. This pattern is important because the morphology is underpinned by a specific relationship between the houses and the street. The house is located within a homestead plot, which comprises the house, the *barge* or backyard land or garden space. Each Santal family typically owns a stretch of land extending from the *kulhi* to backyards and a little beyond. If we consider a transverse section through a family's land, one finds the *kulhi* at one end, followed by the house, the *barge* (backyard) and a stretch of land covered in trees. The extent of tree cover beyond the barge varies. In Bandudih, houses are built very close together and the surrounding areas have been converted into agricultural land to the maximum extent possible. Consequently, the agricultural fields extended up to the *barge* in some cases. In Bhagabondhi, a road was constructed behind the houses and this formed the edge of people's properties. Beyond the row of homestead plots lies the agricultural land. With this distribution and sequence of spaces, it is imperative for every dwelling to be located adjacent to each other in order that they may all have similar access to the *kulhi*.

Houses located in proximity to each other comprise a *tola* or neighbourhoods and most villages usually have more than one *tola* (Figure 5.1). Bandudih, for instance, has three *tolas* named Bandudih, Bhagundih and Taloidih; Bhagabondhi has four *tolas* named Jahira Tola, Mahato Tola, Shankardih, and Dangar Kulhi; while Haudah has four *tolas* named Jahira Tola, Buru Tola, Bulin Tola and Achut Tola. The same *kulhi* winds its way through the different tolas. The *tola* and the *kulhi* are important organising elements within the morphology of the settlement, and as I discuss later, have become synonymous with the neighbourhood itself. These settlements were not planned or built at one time. The *kulhi* as it is today emerged over time with houses being gradually built on either side of it. A comparison of Bondudih and Haudah reveals the process. Jahira Tola in Haudah, even today, has houses built quite far apart, i.e., it has a lower density of building when compared to the other villages such as Bandudih, which is very densely built up. By tracing the growth of extended families and pattern of subdivision of houses and property we can explain how village density increases over time. One family of three brothers lived together in one house in Haudah. In the course of time, one brother got married and built his own house next to his parents' house. Two brothers continued to live together by internally dividing the parents' house for their respective family needs. One of them now has grown-up children. In anticipation of them getting married and requiring more space, he decided to build a separate house. In the course of about 20 years, what was a single house located on a large stretch of land along the *kulhi* became three individual houses built adjacent to each other. Bhagabondhi with densely built up houses presents this future of densification. We also occasionally find empty spots along the *kulhi,* though all other houses are built adjacent to each other. In one such case, this belonged to an

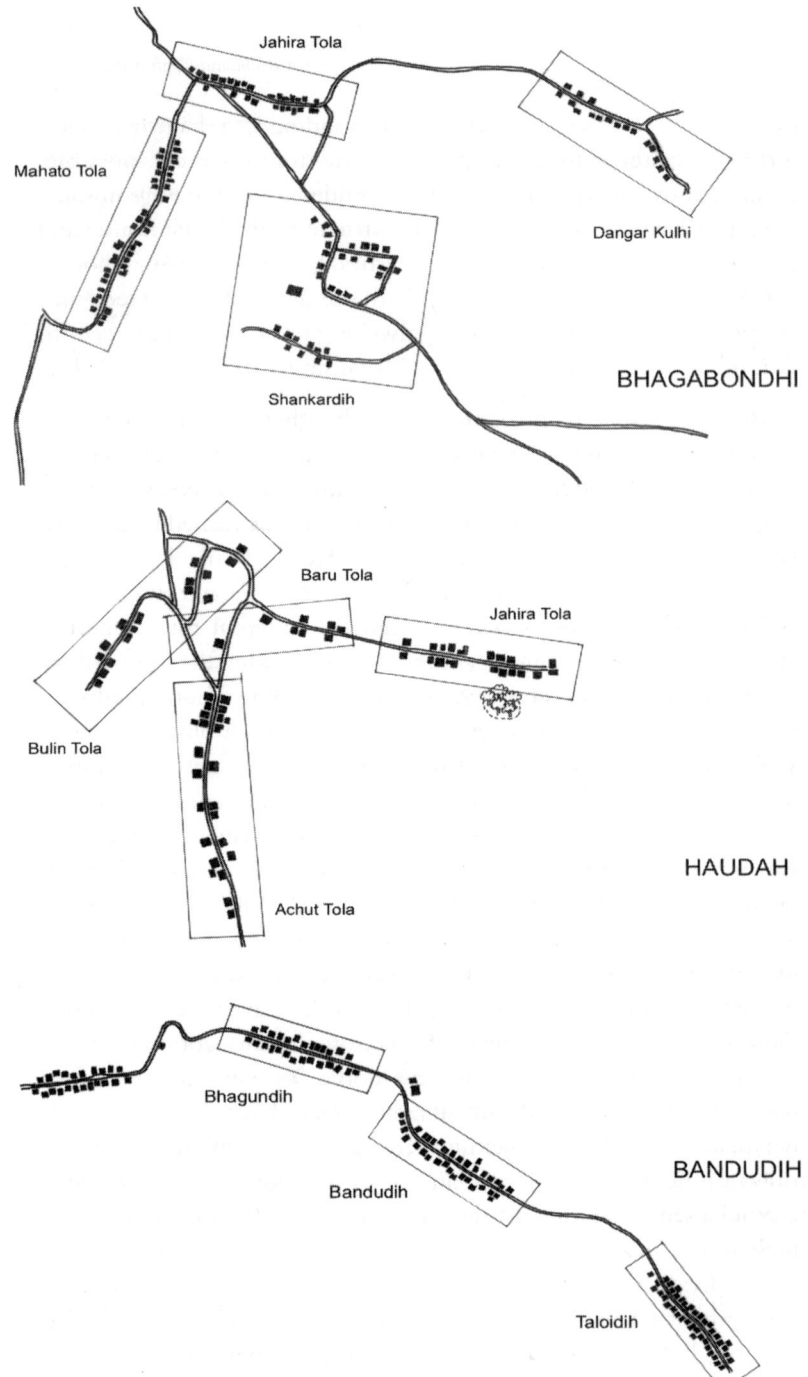

Figure 5.1 Tola *in Different Villages*

extended family where only the younger son remained since his older brother and father died a few years earlier. With no other male members of the family, the need to subdivide the land and build more houses did not arise and consequently, the stretch of land along the *kulhi* remained unoccupied.

These narratives provide vital clues for reimagining the village as it might have existed in the past. In the early days of settlement, rather than houses being built next to each other, from one end of the *kulhi* to the other, large tracts of the land were divided and occupied by families. Houses were interspersed on these stretches of land, and gauging from the distances in Haudah, were very likely to be distant from each other. The path, usually almost linear, that connected these houses, over time became consolidated into the *kulhi*. As families grew, the plots were internally subdivided and more houses built. It is only after two or three generations of house building that the *kulhi* develops as a continuous row of houses on either side, as we see in the villages today. What this pattern of growth suggests is that groups of adjacent houses belong to families of the same lineage, i.e., they may share the same last name. According to myth, all Santals trace their ancestry to seven septs or clans, who are believed to have descended from seven siblings of a mythical ancestral couple, Pilchu Hiram and Pilchu Budhi. Each clan has a totemic animal that they do not harm. Members of the sept usually have the same last name and do not intermarry.[49] So a cluster of houses belonging to members of the same family is also identifiable by the fact that they have a common last name. Family members also refer to each other's houses as being part of their family. During the early days of fieldwork, this was quite confusing for me. Trying to determine the spatial constitution of the house, I would ask which rooms and yards belonged to the family. They would point to neighbouring houses and say that this was all part of the family. It was only much later, when I learnt about extended family structures and property division between them, did the link between these become apparent.

Such clusters of houses are the first level of interaction between the family and the community as a whole. They emerge as important social units within the fabric of the *tola* as kinship structures that become spatialised over time through the addition of houses. This development is clearly rooted in the threshold moment of sedentarisation in the history of the region. In the days of living in the *kumbha*, the frequent moving and reestablishment of dwellings at different sites will have prevented any concretisation of kinship ties in this manner. One of the specific effects of this development is the emergence of networks for women. As such, women are largely bound to the house, both notionally and to a large extent through practice. The families in the vicinity of their own home become an important network that they were a part of. In the previous chapter, I discussed how women artists draw inspirations from each other's designs. In fact, in some villages in purulia, where the women were producing exceptionally detailed designs, there was a clear connection between the murals of the families that were related to each other. One cluster of four or five houses was similarly painted, while the other houses in the *tola* had simple murals. Even though other women in the neighbourhood would have seen each other's designs, it was the closer interaction and conversation between the related families that led the women to discuss designs and produce what may be considered as a coordinated design scheme.

TOPOGRAPHY AND SETTLEMENT

The relative locations of houses, agricultural land, and forests within the village was rooted in family and kinship structure as discussed above, but also in principles of managing water and optimising the undulations of land for various purposes. In terms of spatial distribution, agricultural land is not attached to homestead plots and families may have plots of land located in different places within the village precinct. In villages that have more than one *tola,* agricultural land is spread across the village and families from one *tola* may own land near another *tola.* The spatial distribution of agricultural land does not correspond to the spatial and social groupings within the *tola.* This kind of a physical structure emerges on account of how land was distributed between the members of the community. Land is graded according to its elevation and soil quality, which is linked to its capacity to retain moisture and its suitability for growing paddy. The identification of different types of land for different purposes is directly linked to the form of the village settlement.[50] Homestead plots were located at higher elevations, while agricultural land was identified based on the suitability of land, and this meant that the two were nearly never contiguous.

The linear placement of the houses and the *kulhi* is closely linked to the topography in the Singhbhum region at large. The landscape of Singhbhum is a gently undulating one, comprising elongated ridges. The *kulhi* and houses are located on the lower slopes of the land to ensure the flow of water away from the houses and into the fields. The higher elevation is required, since Singhbhum is a high rainfall region and the mud dwellings need to be protected from the natural flow of water. Dampness is a serious concern for the families. In Haudah, the entire village shifted from a lower to a higher location nearby, for this reason. Villagers recollect that in the past the walls of their houses were constantly damp and this led to an unhealthy living space, as well as a weakened structure. The village council decided to shift the entire *kulhi* elsewhere. The older *kulhi* is visible as a trace in satellite images of the surroundings of the village. Along the length of the *kulhi*, the highest point lies somewhere in the middle, while land begins to slope downwards towards the two ends. Similarly, in the transverse section through the *kulhi*, the higher elevation of the houses compared to the *barge* or the thickets of trees or agricultural land beyond, is perceptible. This specific relationship to topography goes beyond a functional response to landscape and has over time coalesced into place names and the memory of the act of settlement. This is interesting because as a consequence of memorialising the moment of settling, the previous history of migration is also kept alive in cultural memory.

According to the villagers, in the past, groups of men or families set out to find a place to settle and after due ritual processes, identified the location to establish a village. There are no recent memories of villages being newly settled, which is understandable considering that the contemporary geography of land was more or less fixed with colonial tenure and revenue systems, and any possibility of significant migration between places was effectively halted. Elderly villagers in many places recollect hearing from their elders about bands of families moving from one location to another and choosing a site to settle in through divination. If good omens were observed, then the place was considered satisfactory and the group decided to settle.[51] The men first built a small shelter to mark the house of the leader of the group who would become the *manjhi* of the village. The *manjhi* then divided the land among the families within the group. The *naeke* (priest) in the group invited spirits to take up residence at a location of their choice. Through him or other men who went into a trance, the spirits are believed to communicate their will and a particular tree or cluster of trees was then sanctified as the *jahira*. In due course, a second shrine known as the *manjhithan* was established in front of the *manjhi's* house. Other members of the founding group or new families occupied locations along the *kulhi* and built their houses.[52]

The *manjhi's* house together with the houses of the other founders of the village were among the first houses to be built and these were typically located at the highest point of the *kulhi*. One tola in most villages is called Upor Tola or the higher *tola* in direct reference to the elevated topography. This *tola* is nearly always the first site that was settled in the village. It is also often the cluster of houses around the *manjhi's* house. This is because the position of the *manjhi* is a hereditary one and in many villages the *manjhi* continues to belong to the lineage of the person who first founded the village. Consequently, the family continues to live on the same location which is the highest elevation locally. In some cases, the *manjhi's* house was not located at the highest point or the approximate centre of the village. In these cases, villagers had appointed a new *manjhi* from a different family, usually due to some problem in leadership. The name Upor Tola continued to perpetuate the memory of the original settling of the village.

The elevated location of the *manjhi's* house and the first place of settlement, are common in villages of Adivasi communities other than Santals as well. In Bandudih, the headman of the village is a Munda and the cluster around his house is also referred to as the Upor Tola. What distinguishes Santals, however, is that the settling of the village is further commemorated through the *manjhithan*. After the *jahira*, this is the most important ritual location in the village (Figure 5.2). It is a shrine dedicated to the ancestral headman, i.e., ancestors belonging to the *manjhi's* lineage and is located in front of the *manjhi's* house on the *kulhi*. As in the case of the location of the *manjhi's* house, the

Figure 5.2 Manjhithan

manjhithan too was moved to other locations, in recent times, for various reasons. In Haudah, the *manjhithan* had been intentionally shifted to a location that was more central in relation to the different *tolas* of the village. The new location was adjacent to a large ground rather than to any house to allow people to gather for community-level ritual activities. In another village, Bangoda, the community elected a new *manjhi* in place of the person who inherited the position from his father. Consequently, the *manjhithan* was shifted to the front of the new *manjhi*'s house, which lay towards one end of the *kulhi*. In Bandudih, there was a sizeable population of Santals who lived together with Mundas and Gops, but there was no *manjhithan* in the village. This is because the original settlers were Mundas, who claim that they invited Santals to settle in their midst. The Mundas themselves were migrants replacing Hos, who were the first settlers of the village. In recent years, however, Santals had appointed their own *manjhi* in addition to the Munda headman and had also established their own *jahira*. They did not, however, establish a *manjhithan*, presumably on account of the fact that they are not the first people to settle in that place. Orans makes a similar point regarding Santal families who migrated to urban areas and lived in houses provided by their employers, which was very common especially in industrial and mining companies during this period. In such cases, he found that Santal families did not designate a space as a *bhitar*, since they were not sure of the spirits who may have previously resided in those houses. This suggests that commemorating the act of settling and invoking the protection of spirits and ancestors is only done when a community settles in a place that was previously unoccupied.[53] Also, the *manjhithan* is as much a shrine of ancestral headmen as it is a memorial to the act of settling in the village. This explains why changing village politics may produce a new head but this does not always lead to the establishment of the *manjhithan* as an attendant institution.

The *manjhithan*, as a register of the connection between a Santal community, their place of inhabitation and the past, is very different from the Munda registers of belonging. Munda villages have a place known as *sasandhiri* where the bones of deceased members from a particular lineage are buried. The *sasandhiri* comprises large slabs of stone below which the bones are buried (Figure 5.3). *Sasandhiri* may be of two kinds: a large burial site with a number of stones and bones of many members of a particular lineage, or a single stone placed at the entrance of individual Munda houses, where bones of an immediate family member who is deceased are buried. It is important to note here that lineage among Mundas is traced through the male line but belonging is premised on birth. So Munda women continue to belong to their father's lineage even after marriage. In case of death, the body is cremated but the bones returned to the paternal village to be buried in the *sasan dhiri* there. This is very different from the custom among Santals, where one's lineage depends upon the relationship with male relatives; so Santal women belong to the father's lineage while single, and then to the husband's lineage after marriage. Unlike the Mundas,

Figure 5.3 Sasandhiri, *The Burial Place of Munda Families*

where women remain connected to the paternal *sasandhiri*, married Santal women do not have access to the *bhitar* in their father's house. The collective *sasandhiri* particularly becomes an important point of connection and reference for belonging to a place on account of the fact that subsequent generations of Mundas may be buried there. This is in fact the pillar on the basis of which Mundas claim ownership of land. In comparison, Santal ways of establishing a connection with a place are primarily premised on the successful invocation of the protective influence of spirits and deceased ancestors, and having access to the shrines where the spirits are believed to reside. This point is developed further when I discuss spatial definitions of *tolas* vis-à-vis social sub-groupings of community through the idea of protective spirit domains.

To return to the earlier point about Santals not establishing shrines at places that have been previously settled by some other community, as in the case in Bandudih, where Santal members of the village built their own *jahira* but not a *manjhithan*, I suggested that this was on account of a fear of other spirits who may be residing there and who may or may not be benevolent towards new settlers. This idea resonated with stories of people's movements and settling of villages that were shared by a number of villagers as I found during my fieldwork. One of the most common terms people used to describe settling in a place was that it 'suited' the families. My fieldwork conversations typically took place in Hindi, but people used the English word 'suit' to describe people's affiliations to places they settled in. In Bandudih, people remember Hos as being the first settlers of the village. In fact, Ho memories persist through large memorial stones, which the current residents attribute to Ho people living here in the past. This is likely, since Hos are the only Adivasi community associated with a megalithic culture, at least in the past, if not today.[54] The *devi*—goddess worshipped in the *devisthal* that is the most sacred site in the village—did not suit the Hos. They eventually left the village and Munda families gradually moved in. That the *devi* is protective towards Mundas is expressed through incidents such as an attack by a colonial official in the past, who came on horseback with a battalion of soldiers. As the officer tried to enter the village precinct, he was thrown off his horse and the villagers believe it was the *devi* who made this happen in order to protect them. Similarly, in two other villages that have only Santal families as residents, villagers believe that the village does not suit people from other communities. In both cases they mentioned that when people from other communities tried to settle in this village, they were warned away by an old man who troubled them in their dreams. In narrating these beliefs, villagers mentioned that they could not precisely identify what these powers were or why others could not settle in particular places; in fact, they maintained that there was something inexplicable about such incidents. What is interesting is that in spite of the differences in how communities register their connections to a place, they all invoke divine sanction as legitimising their presence in a particular location on the one hand and the absence of other communities on the other.

KULHI AND COMMUNITY

The spatial organisation of Santal houses reinforces the centrality of the *kulhi* in the social life of the community. Each family builds their house directly on the *kulhi*, i.e., their front door leads straight to the street.

Some villagers explained this as a ritual requirement. When a family member dies, their body must be taken out of the house through the front door. Since the deceased eventually join the rank of spirits to be worshipped, and each house is the abode of spirits, it is inappropriate for the body to be taken across somebody else's house. Should houses be located behind one another, the passage of the dead body may pass through another family's courtyard and this may disrupt the journey of the deceased into the spirit world on account of the influence of other domestic spirits. Once the body has been buried or cremated, a piece of bone from the forehead is sealed in a clay pot with a hole in the lid. This pot contains the spirit of the deceased ancestor. When the family returns to the village with the pot, they stop at the entrance to the village and build a small shed representing a house. The pot is placed inside and offerings are made to the spirit. The shed is then burnt and the family members call out to the spirit saying that the house is burning down, and so they should come to reside in their house instead. In this manner, spirits of deceased ancestors are ritually invited to take up residence in the *bhitar*.[55] For this reason, too, it is important to have a clear passage between the *kulhi* and the house so that the spirit can make their way into the house.

The physical proximity of the families living in a particular *tola* binds them into definite everyday social relations with one another. In the previous chapter, I discussed that women plaster the *kulhi racha* or the part of the *kulhi* in front of their house twice or three times a week with cow dung and thus the entire *kulhi* is well maintained. These acts are gestures of collective responsibility towards the *kulhi* as a public space. Similarly, water flows are managed to ensure that it does not sully the *kulhi*. Locals, both Adivasis and non–Adivasis, often referred to this point about water management and cleanliness when describing key characteristics of Santal settlements. All washing activities for instance are carried out in the *barge*, or in some cases inside the *racha* with a drain leading to the back. As discussed before, in villages where communities are internally in conflict or under any kind of stress, the collective maintenance of the *kulhi* is hampered. As a corollary, the collective practices of maintaining the *kulhi* serve to enforce a sense of community among the residents as well. Interestingly, *kulhi* is a generic word used to describe the central street in other Adivasi villages as well.

However, the meticulous maintenance, the direct access of every house to the *kulhi,* and its relationship to community solidarity is a uniquely Santal attribute. In villages where Santals lived together with other Adivasi and non-Adivasi families, some of these traits of Santal settlements are modified or no longer present. In Bandudih for instance, a few houses are located behind each other and women plaster only a small area demarcating their *kulhi* racha rather than covering the entire street, which is the case in Bhagabondhi where only Santals live.

Occasionally one finds houses built at a distance from the *kulhi.* These houses may belong to people who have been ostracised from the community. When I asked about the people living there the villagers did not give any clear answers. A typical response to my question was that the person living there was *pagal* or mad, that they may not interest me and I should ignore the house. It is likely that these houses belonged to ostracised families, or at least those who for some reason are not part of the community. Literature on Santal rituals provides details of the *bitlaha* or ostracisation ceremony, where defiling the house plays an important role. Somers notes that during these events, the house of the family to be ostracised was broken into and defiled in various ways such as by breaking and burning, in addition to the family being made to leave the village.[56] Most villagers were not very willing to discuss these matters and so it is not clear as to what is the nature of the *bitlaha* today. What was evident was that the practices of ostracisation vary. In the villages I visited, the punishments are less severe and families are typically prohibited from having any interactions with other members of the village community. In cases where families are ostracised but their houses are already part of the *kulhi,* rather than being asked to leave or the house being damaged, other forms of sanction are imposed. I noted this in two cases in Bhagabondhi. In the first case, a man was polygamous and had remarried multiple times in spite of repeated injunctions from the village council to not do so. However, the man was a timber contractor, and supplied wood to neighbouring cities. He was relatively wealthy and employed many men from the village. His economic position within the community made it difficult to ostracise him completely or to ask him to move out of his home. Consequently, he was punished by not being allowed to participate in ritual activity in the *jahira.* In another example, members within a family were accused of murdering another family member. After due legal process against the two accused members, it was decided that other members of the community would not interact with the family as a whole. The family left the village soon after this incident and returned a year later, but the sanctions against interacting with them remained in force. The important point here is that living on the *kulhi* is an important marker of membership within a community, and the proximity binds families into consensual norms of behaviour and practice. However, there are social and economic complexities, together with contemporary forms of land and house ownership, which prevent the absolute removal of families from the neighbourhood and community.

In comparison to Santal houses, Munda houses are not always directly located on the *kulhi*, though they also maintain ritual connections with the *kulhi* for death-related rites as described earlier (Figure 5.4). Munda women establish this connection by plastering a path from the front door to the *kulhi* using cow dung during the weekly plastering activity. These paths are often sinuous and weave their way around other dwellings but they ensure that a notional connection is established with the *kulhi* and that it does not cross the courtyard or entrance of any other house on the way. If this is impossible on account of the location of other houses, a patch is plastered in front of their house such that it is broadly oriented towards the *kulhi*. Santal houses nearly never resort to such improvisations and take care to build their houses with orthogonal geometries that ensure direct access. Both Mundas and Santals remain connected to the *kulhi* and they both plaster the *kulhi racha*, but the form and the signification of the connection varies.

In the previous chapter I discussed how *alpana*, floor drawings made with rice flour, are typically understood as a Hindu practice rather than an Adivasi one, but some Santal and other Adivasi families have adopted it under varying circumstances. *Alpana* designs are typically made on the *kulhi* during the weekly plastering activity and in front of the *tulsi pinda* (mud platform with sacred plant) within the *racha* of the house. Two kinds of *alpana* designs are distinguishable: those with ritual significance and those that appear to largely serve a decorative purpose. Designs with ritual significance are made by dipping a finger in rice paste and tracing lines with that finger. The motifs are

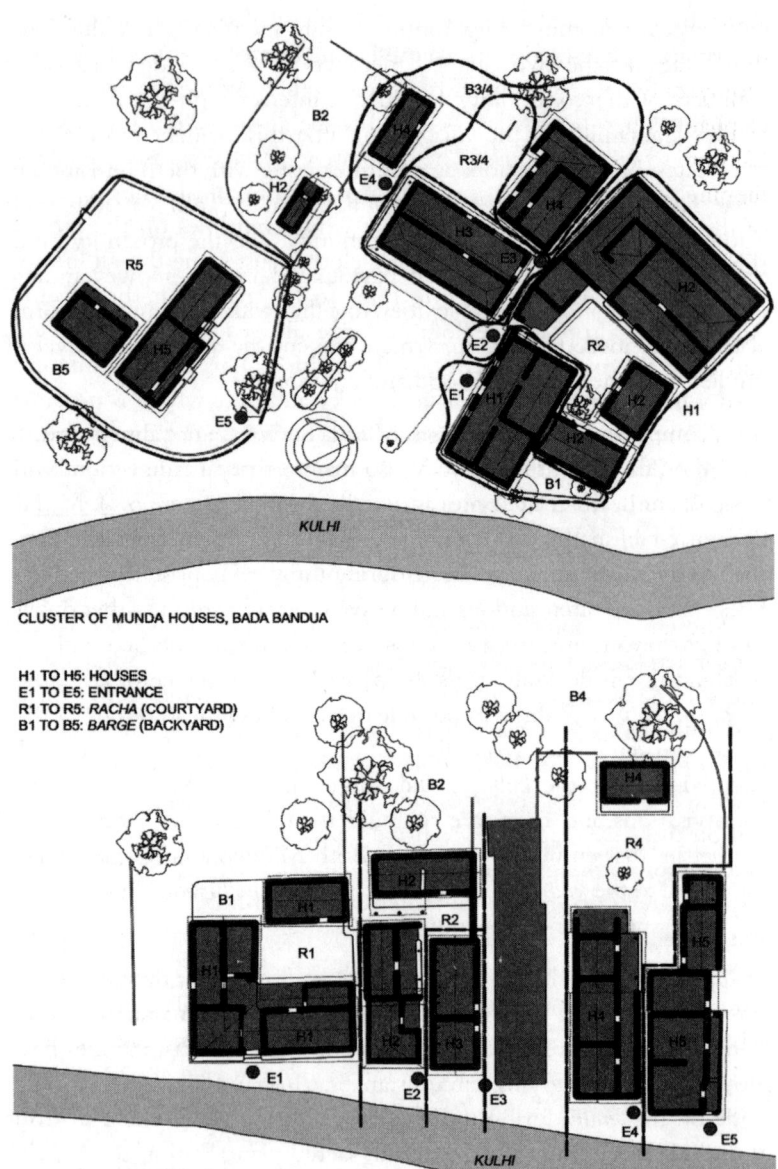

CLUSTER OF MUNDA HOUSES, BADA BANDUA

H1 TO H5: HOUSES
E1 TO E5: ENTRANCE
R1 TO R5: *RACHA* (COURTYARD)
B1 TO B5: *BARGE* (BACKYARD)

CLUSTER OF SANTAL HOUSES, BADA BANDUA

Figure 5.4 *Comparison of Santal and Munda House Clusters*

abstractions of Hindu deities such as Goddess Laksmi and take the form of triangular or stylised shapes representing her feet. Women also commonly draw sets of concentric circles representing the feet of the elephant. These motifs are believed to be an invitation for Goddess Lakshmi to visit the house. The decorative *alpana* designs are made by dipping a piece of cloth into a thin rice paste and trailing one end of the cloth on the ground to leave white thin lines on the ground (Figure 5.5). The trailing end of the cloth is just some thread in most cases and this allows very fine lines to be traced on the ground. Alternatively, drops of rice flour paste are allowed to drip off the cloth and lines are made as a series of these drips. This drip technique is used when women do not have a sticky additive, which is procured from plants available in the vicinity of the village. The designs traced by finger have thicker lines as compared to those made by trailing a piece of cloth. In terms of motifs too some differences are evident. The decorative *alpana* present a range of floral patterns and other patterns that do not have a clear religious symbolism.

Though the motifs and techniques described above are largely similar across the villages where *alpana* is made, there are some differences in the overall design in relation to the demography of the village and to the patterns of use and association with the *kulhi*. In Bandudih, the *alpana* is drawn such that it has a border that frames it from all sides (Figure 5.6). In Bhagabondhi, the *alpana* is larger and appears to spread out on the *kulhi* (Figure 5.7). If we consider the extent of the *alpana* as a way of marking territory, then the *alpana* with a border indicates a specific territory, while the other designs do not. This difference is not an accident of design, but a specific response to the space of the *kulhi* itself. In Bandudih, the *kulhi* is culturally shared between Mundas, Santals and Gop families and collective practices vacillate between the taboos of the different communities at various points in time. The *kulhi* is a shared but contested space. Additionally, the *kulhi* has turned into a thoroughfare that heavy vehicles use to access stone quarries that lie beyond the village. These usages have detracted from the sense of the *kulhi* as an institution and it was clearly on the verge of becoming a more impersonal road. In this context, the framed *alpana* designs indicated the extent to which each household claims part of the *kulhi*, and conversely, they also indicate the lack of personalisation of the rest of

Figure 5.5 Alpana *with a Line Extending Along the Slope Indicating a House's Connection with the* Kulhi

the *kulhi* space. In Bhagabondhi, on the other hand, *alpana* designs tend to spread out on the *kulhi* in both size and design. The *kulhi* has only Santal houses, it is well maintained through regular plastering, and as such functions as an important social institution. The *alpana* in such

Figure 5.6 Alpana *with a Border Marking the Extent of a House's Claim to the* Kulhi

cases only indicates the threshold into the house but does not necessarily delineate the territory of the *kulhi racha*. The difference between a design with a border and one without may appear very nominal but is indicative of the subtle but clear difference in perceptions of the *kulhi*.

Figure 5.7 Alpana *without Borders*

This idea of the *alpana* as an index of access to the *kulhi* was clearly illustrated in one particular munda dwelling, where four brothers lived in a single courtyard house located at a considerable distance from the *kulhi*. There was only one entrance to this house but each family needed to distinguish their own space for ritual purposes. Consequently, an *alpana* line was drawn from the entrance into the courtyard of the house. This line then split into three and led to different *tulsi pindas* and doors leading to each of the brothers' sections. The *alpana* in this case served to define different houses, their internal sacred geographies through the connection between the front doors, and the different *tulsi pindas*, and also distinguish between the families' individual claims to the *kulhi* under circumstances when these differences could not be spatially made.

KULHI AS A SPACE OF RITUAL PROTECTION

The *manjhithan* is the ritual centre of the Santal *kulhi*. Located opposite the house of the *manjhi*, it ranges from being marked with a single log of wood with a few stones embedded near the base to a permanent pavilion-like structure. As the shrine is dedicated to the ancestral headmen of the village, it is an important site of worship for the village community. It is also an important place in everyday life, since it is considered to be the abode of *manjhibaba*, a spirit representing the headman's lineage and who extends protection to those living in the *kulhi*. In Phulgoda, villagers believe that if someone is travelling at night, *manjhibaba* accompanies them as they walk along the *kulhi* up to the edge of the village. On ritual occasions such as marriages, the wedding party or the returning groom and bride seek the blessings of *manjhibaba* upon their entry into the village. Apart from these ritual occasions, there are a number of taboos on particular kinds of activities in the *kulhi* on account of the fact that it is considered a domain of ancestral headmen and other spirits. Troisi suggests that these practices and taboos notionally demarcate the *kulhi* as a domain under the protective influence of spirits.[57]

If the *manjhithan* marks the ritual centre, there must also be a limit to this protective domain. It is the boundary beyond which the protective influence of *manjhibaba* does not continue to extend and where does a *kulhi* end. One indicator of this boundary is suggested by rituals of departure from the village. During wedding ceremonies for instance, when the groom and his family leave for the bride's village, other villagers accompany them as they move through the village. At one point, which is considered as the end of the *kulhi*, the *manjhi* sits down and the wedding party seek his blessings before moving on. This moment and place are suggestive of the end of the village and the gesture of seeking blessings from the *manjhi* is an extension of seeking protection from the ancestral spirits as the wedding party is now moving beyond their protective sphere. Similarly, in the case of deaths, there are certain markers and rites specific to the end of the village. In Bandudih, villagers said that in case of somebody's death, an upturned cart is placed at one end of the *kulhi* to inform visitors that the space of the village is now ritually polluted. In the case of funeral rites as I discussed in the previous chapter, a small house is made for the deceased spirit at one end of the *kulhi*. In all these cases, there is a distinction being made between the inside and the outside of a village through the *kulhi*. The threshold is not physically marked but becomes established through ritual practices alone. The end of the *kulhi* is conversely suggested as a threshold beyond which the villager is outside the protective influence of *manjhibaba*.

It is important to point out here that the end of a *kulhi* is different from the limits of *tola* since the same *kulhi* winds through different *tolas* in a village. The limits of a *kulhi* correspond to what may be considered as the end of the village, while the limits of a *tola* vacillate between administrative and social definition. I discussed earlier that clusters within the *tola* are formed by houses of families belonging to the same lineage and are an important arena of social interaction for women. What was interesting was that these clusters are identifiable sub-units for others as well. During a conversation with a group of children in Haudah, they said that they did not know much about or interact with children living further down the same *tola*. This was surprising since the groups of houses where the children played were located less than 100 metres from each other and children are as such used to travelling across the landscape to various parts of the village. Unlike women who have limited mobility in everyday life, children's movements are not restricted. At the very least children walk past each other's houses on their way to school. So, when they claimed to only play with other children from the immediate vicinity of their own homes and not with those living in other clusters, one can assume a correlation between the spatial and social subgroups within the *tola*. Even as a whole, the *tola* itself is a complex entity. Morphologically speaking, it is a proximal cluster of houses and is usually distinctly located from other clusters along the same kulhi. However, the *tola* does not necessarily end where the houses do. For instance, in the Jahira Tola in Bhagabondi, the houses extended for a considerable distance, but women referred to a point approximately midway, suggested by the location of a well, as being the end of the tola. This limit was a clearly social one. Families who lived within the limits identified by the women, had reciprocal relationships with each other. They were obligated to invite and attend events such as weddings in each other's families. The families living beyond the point indicated by the women were physically proximal to and were part of the village as a whole but were not considered as part of the *tola* community. So the physical proximity of houses within a cluster or presence in the *kulhi* does not automatically imply a community at the level of a *tola* since ritual participation is an intersecting factor as well.

VILLAGE AS BOUNDED SPACE, VILLAGE AS COMMUNITY

In discussing the morphology of Santal settlements, I mentioned that homestead plots are located along the *kulhi*, while agricultural lands are distributed at various places within the village precinct in relation to topography. The village boundary is not apparent in everyday life but is important considering that it is the only container of distributed agricultural and other lands that comprise the village as an administrative unit. For this reason, it is a sensitive issue for villagers, which I realised when I enquired about land ownership during fieldwork. While villagers offered general descriptions about the nature of agricultural lands and their relative productivity, they shared no specific information about land ownership. In two instances, people showed me revenue maps, which are documents produced by the State to indicate the extents of the village but declined my requests to copy the information. I was told that this was sensitive information and villagers were reluctant to share it with outsiders. This reluctance is partly historical given the record of Adivasis' alienation from their lands in Singhbhum and the Chotanagpur region. Villagers continue to remain cautious even today because instances of illegal purchase or occupation of Adivasi lands by non-Adivasis continues. In one case, in the vicinity of Haudah village, some land from the neighbouring village was sold to an industrial establishment, which began constructing a factory on the site. The residents of Haudah were deeply concerned since similar developments in violation of the Chhotanagpur Tenancy Act had occurred in the past and the villagers' protests had not resulted in anything since the factories continued to operate. Such establishments are worrisome because once a piece of land is acquired, the new owners continue to acquire adjoining pieces of land and soon a large number of Adivasi families are left without agricultural land, and therefore without any means to earn a livelihood. While Singhbhum has a long history of wage labour, agricultural land continues to be a source of food and economic security for Adivasi families. The history of conflict around land has made the village boundary an important marker of an 'inside' vis-à-vis the 'outside'. Compared to the ritual boundary markers which operate at the level of the *tola,* the administrative boundaries impose a sense of community among the villagers in relation to the outside world.

Within the village too, land ownership provides insights into understanding the nature of the village community on two counts. Different Adivasi communities have different systems of land ownership and legislation. Santals, for instance, follow a Manjhi Parganait system, while Mundas follow the Munda Manki system.[58] In the case of multi-community villages where non-Adivasis and Adivasis live together, different systems of land ownership and legislation may coexist. This has an impact on both the community and the landscape of the village. In Bhagabondi, Santals live together with Mahato families who do not come under the purview of the Chotanagpur Tenancy Act. Consequently, these families are able to sell their land to other non-Adivasis. Two families had converted their paddy fields into brick kilns. In Bada Bandua, a Gop villager had established a brick kiln in his own paddy field. This obviously affected paddy cultivation in general as the fields are in the form of terraces and interconnected through water flows across the terrain. The wider impact is that the brick kilns often employ other villagers, who may not have agricultural land of their own or whose cultivation may be insufficient for their financial needs. In such cases, the kilns become places of considerable economic importance within the village community. Families who operate the kilns come to wield considerable social status as well. This is similar to the case of the timber trader in Bhagabondi, who could not be ostracised from the village since he provided employment to a number of people in the village. The differences in land legislation and the economic opportunities afforded by the sale or industrial development of land have been leading to shifts in the social dynamics within village communities.

While the village boundary and notions of property evoke a certain sense of community in relation to outsiders, an important register of community within the village is the *jahira*. Simply put, all men who own land within the village must participate in ritual events in the *jahira*. In many cases, men may not own land but cultivate somebody else's land. They too participate in ritual activities and are considered members of the community. The history of migration due to non-agricultural livelihoods has transformed this system in complex ways. In Haudah, villagers defined participation as making monetary contributions towards and participating in ritual events in the *jahira*. They further mentioned that when families migrate, but continue to own agricultural property in the village, they remain obligated to making contributions towards the *jahira* events. In Bhagabondi, in the account of ostracisation that I mentioned earlier, the accused man was prohibited from participating in rituals in the *jahira* and this was considered notionally equivalent to leaving the village, or at least being outside the community. Membership in the *jahira* is traced not only through physical presence in the village and participation in ritual events, but through a notional presence on account of land ownership in the village.

In the case of villages where different communities live together, there are sacred groves belonging to different communities. Bandudih has a Munda *devisthal*, which is considered the primary place of worship in the village, where both Mundas and Santals participate in ritual activity. However, Santal families also perform rituals in a separate *jahira*. This difference emerges on account of the fact that Mundas were the original settlers and therefore their place of worship became the most important ritual location and the marker of community membership as discussed above. Haudah presents another variation. The area traditionally considered to be the Haudah village became divided into two revenue villages of Haudah and the neighbouring Tildih in the course of administrative reorganisation. The division occurred when a railway line was constructed through the village and divided the village into two parts. Since both villages have Santal families, a new *jahira* was established in Tildih. However, since all families earlier belonged to Haudah, they continued to participate in worship at the Haudah *jahira* even after the formation of Tildih. Families in Tildih contribute to and participate in both *jahira,* though families in Haudah are not involved with the Tildih *jahira* in any way. Two points are interesting here. First, even while participating in the Santal *jahira* is important for community membership, the primary affiliation for all Adivasi villagers lies with the first *jahira, devisthal* or other ritual location established within the village. Second, the practice of tracing community affiliation through the *jahira* is stronger among Santals as compared to other Adivasi communities. During conversations about important places within the village, Santal villagers in most places were unanimous about the *jahira* as being the most important site. They explained it as the equivalent of the Hindu temple. Munda villagers were not as insistent about their *devisthal* being the most important part of the village. While this is not an absolute statement about the relative importance of the sacred grove to the respective communities, it does indicate, locally if not universally, a cultural difference in place association.

Community is not a stable formation. Adivasi communities are of varied types, as social and spatial agglomerations negotiated through places and practices at different scales. At the dwelling-cluster level, it is the women and children whose movements indicate a social group; at the *tola* level the practices in the *kulhi* and the *manjhithan* become community identifiers for Santals; while village-level notions of community are negotiated through ritual sites and administrative boundaries between Santals and other communities. It is important to reiterate, however, that these notions have emerged in the interplay with various other factors such as practices of other communities, intra-village politics, and administrative organisation and reorganisation. In short, Santal communities emerge through complex networks of affinities that include memories of settling, responses to topography, establishing protective domains of spirits, and tacit limits of mobility. These are largely anchored within the geography of the *kulhi* as a shared public place.

I unexpectedly encountered this during my interactions with village children. During fieldwork, children were curious about the notes and drawings that I made. I shared some paper with them and asked them to make images of their house or village. The instructions were intentionally broad to allow children to interpret and draw what they considered as constitutive of the house and village, and things they considered important in their environment. For instance, when children have drawn the entire village or picked a view that shows more than one house, the *kulhi* was the key organising element in the drawing and all the other elements were positioned in relation to the *kulhi*. In one example, bends in the *kulhi* indicated different *tola* and in each segment, the child artist wrote the names of the different *tola* in the village. Given that children invent 'pictorial equivalents' or 'structurally

Figure 5.8 *Drawing of Village by a Ten-year-old Boy*

Note the labels in each segment of the road, which refer to the names of different *tola* in the village

adequate forms which can stand for a complex object,' in these draw-ings, the children visualised the spatial units of the village in reference to the *kulhi* (Figure 5.8).[59] Clearly, the imagination of community is multivalent, not just as the result of academic analysis but in the experiences and perceptions of the villagers themselves.

Chapter 6

Domestic Space, Mobility and Patterns of Everyday Life

Place, as a concept, is as much a spatial construct as it is a process of inhabitation. Adivasi families traverse the landscape far beyond their village in pursuit of livelihood, domestic chores, to visit markets, their extended families, and for ritual hunting, to name just a few activities. Further, men and women have different mobility patterns and distinctly different engagements with and perceptions of the village and its environments. In direct contrast to the spatially bounded house and village are the complex and fluid networks of interaction between Adivasi families and various Adivasi and non-Adivasi neighbours, the industrialising rural landscape, and the small and large urban centres across Singhbhum. The previous chapters offered an illustration of how these networks of interactivity percolate into everyday life, and in the form of design developments in mural art. I now discuss these networks not just as a context for understanding the transformation of built environments but as fundamentally inscribing the larger landscape of Adivasi inhabitation.

In tracing the mobility of individuals, it is imperative to distinguish between men and women since their respective mobilities are underpinned by different social roles, cultural norms, and economic opportunities. Gender played an important role in my own presence in the village and access to the community. When first introduced to the villagers, I expressed my interest in the house and everyday life of the family. This inadvertently gendered emphasis channelised my questions to women as the people responsible for the dwellings as well as domestic responsibilities. Men were also curious about my work and would interact with me, but usually left after asking preliminary questions about who I was and what I was doing. People who introduced me to the village, and to other men in the village, directed my questions to women saying that they could tell me whatever I wanted to know about domestic life. My own background as a wife, mother, daughter-in-law and a teacher made women rather than men interested in knowing more about my family, which in turn led to further conversations. For instance, women were very curious about how my children were being looked after when I was away for fieldwork, who cooked in my family, and what my husband and father-in-law did for a living. Consequently, I developed a more empathetic relationship with women, which allowed me to construct detailed ethnographies of subsistence production and domestic work. At the level of the settlement and the community, matters took a distinctively gendered socio-political turn. I asked questions about issues such as land division, institutions, and the sacred geography of the village, all of which fall within a more male domain of knowledge. It took multiple conversations with different men to glean some insights into these aspects of village life. Limitations notwithstanding, what was apparent was that men and women have distinctly different patterns of movement through and across the village, and these present a very different picture of habitations as evoked through gendered everyday movements. I focus particularly on the activities, mobility and awareness of Santal women, and explore various dimensions of their relationship with the lived environment in terms of networks of everyday life and dwelling thresholds.

BOUND TO HOME AND HEARTH?

The first task of the day for women, as discussed in the previous chapter, is to ritually purify the house by applying a patch of cow dung on the floor at all the entrances. Once this is done, women collect water from the nearest tap, well or hand pump and begin preparing the first meal of the day. This comprises tea, rice and occasionally some vegetables. The consumption of vegetables varied significantly depending on a family's capacity to grow or buy them. Rice however was a staple and Santals consumed it in the form of *madh bhat*, which is rice cooked with a lot of water resulting in a porridge-like preparation. According to the villagers, this form of rice kept the body hydrated while they went about their work during the day. Other members of the family eat soon after the meal is prepared. Men and women do not eat together as it is considered taboo.[60] Men eat first while women are at hand to serve since it is not considered appropriate for a person to serve themselves while eating. The timings of these activities vary (Table 6.1) depending upon whether women are employed elsewhere as wage

Table 6.1 *Summary of the Daily Routine of Women in Santal Households in the Case Study Villages*

Time of day	Tasks performed by women
4:00–8:00 am	• Wake up, apply cow dung patches to entrances, collect water, cook morning meals, eat. • Leave for work (for women employed as wage labourers).
8:00–10:00 am	• Let cattle out of shelters and give them feed and water, cattle taken away/ let out for grazing. • Clean the cattle shelter and rest of the house; plaster *kulhi racha* and house twice a week.
10:00 am–12:00 pm	Varying activities by women in different villages: • Make excursions to collect wood (Observed in Chauda) • Gather cow dung (Observed in Bada Bandua) • Prepare *handia* (rice beer) (Observed in Bhagabandh in the house of M.Hansdah where she ran the village handia shop) • Other preparations such as par-boiling paddy and pounding paddy for extraction of rice.
12:00–2:00 pm	Bathing, washing clothes, eating second meal of the day, washing utensils.
2:00–4:00 pm	Complete odd jobs around the house/rest, animals return from grazing and are fed, given water and moved into their shelters for the night.
4:00–6:00 pm	Collect water, cook last meal of the day, eat, wash utensils and clean up.
6:00–8:00 pm	(Not observed) relaxing/ chatting until they go to sleep.

labourers, in which case, they begin these activities before dawn and leave for work by 7 am in the morning. If women do not work elsewhere, the next task after cooking and eating is to let cattle out of their shelters and give them fodder and water. By 9 am approximately, the cattle are taken away for grazing by another member of the family or an outsider employed for that purpose. The arrangements for cattle grazing vary across villages depending on the employment of women. In Bhagabondi, for instance, one elderly couple in the village took the cattle from a few houses to graze collectively and each family paid the couple in cash or kind. In Haudah, each family sent one person, usually a young boy, out with the cattle. When no one was available, the cattle were let out into a large fenced area near the house for the whole day. In Bandudih, the arrangements varied across families since many families did not have cattle at all. Once the cattle leave, women begin the task of cleaning the house. This includes cleaning out the rooms where the cattle are sheltered, sweeping the entire house, and plastering the interiors and the *kulhi racha* twice or three times a week.

During the mid-morning hours, i.e., after cleaning and before noon, women carry out a range of activities, which vary across villages. During the agricultural season, this may be the time women and children go to work in the paddy fields. Men typically leave for the fields soon after eating the first meal of the day in the morning. In Bhagabondi, women and young girls followed cattle to collect cow dung, prepared *handia* (rice beer) or go to collect wood from nearby forests, depending upon what their immediate requirements were. In Haudah, the women who stayed at home during the day stocked up on household essentials such as firewood. This was a time-intensive enterprise and women had to walk a considerable distance to reach a forest. So they preferred these hours to chop and gather large quantities of wood that they then stored for later use. In Bandudih, women spent these hours collecting cow dung, carrying out repairs in the house and preparing *handia*. They did not go to gather wood since the forests are very far from the village and require nearly eight to 10 hours of travel and work. What is evident is that these hours are used by women to carry out a range of activities pertaining to procuring household essentials.

Around noon, women visit the village pond to bathe and wash clothes. Most villagers are particular about the need to bathe before lunch. After bathing, they typically fetch water for the afternoon and then proceed with lunch and washing. Women may then get some rest or continue with activities that remained incomplete in the morning, until the cattle return between 3:00 pm and 4:00 pm. Once they do, they are first given some feed and water. They are led into their shelters and tied up for the night. Before dusk, women begin preparing the evening meal, which again comprises rice and vegetables. They eat at dusk and after cleaning up, their household chores are completed for the day.

The daily life of men is in direct contrast to that of the women. During the agricultural cycle, they are involved in ploughing, preparing the field, planting and harvesting. I visited the villages mostly between January and April, when there is a break in the agricultural season. During these months, men were involved in a wide range of activities depending upon their economic condition. If men were largely involved in wage labour, then the break in the agricultural season did not make a difference to their daily cycles, whereas for paddy cultivators, the months between January and April offered time for miscellaneous jobs or to engage in wage labour to supplement their incomes. In Bandudih and Haudah, most men were involved in wage labour and were rarely present in the village when I visited it. A few men were found in the village, but they were often the elderly or those with ill health. There were also a few others, usually chronic alcoholics, who stayed in the village all the time. Compared to women who had a definite and demanding daily routine, men had vastly varying schedules and often spent large amounts of time on the *kulhi* in conversation with other men. In fact, women unanimously observed that they work more than men, who as they pointed out and I could observe in every village, usually sit around on the *kulhi*.

MOBILITY AND RESOURCE NETWORKS

Water, fuel, and cow dung are some of the basic necessities for which women make daily or frequent trips both within and beyond the village. Women fetch water three or four times a day from wells or hand pumps nearest to their homes. Wells and hand pumps are the only source of water in most villages and groups of 10 to 12 houses may share a well or hand pump between them. Jahira Tola in Bhagabondi was an exception, as it had a deep borewell connected to an overhead tank from where water was distributed to different taps in the *kulhi*. Water was released from the overhead tank twice or three times a day and women collected it at those times. Additionally, there were two wells located at the two ends of the *tola*. Interestingly, the taps and the wells are not open for use by anybody in the village. Rather they are used by specific groups of houses in the immediate vicinity. The allocation of access to water sources was fixed. The only time when the pattern of use changed was when the pump in the borewell broke down for some reason and women had to use the wells until the pump was repaired. In such cases, the normal allocation was not enforced and women collected water from the nearest well or even from wells and taps that were further off, depending on where water was available. In Haudah and Bandudih, water was supplied through hand pumps (tube wells) or collected from village ponds, but the rationale of fixed groups of users remained. The designation of access to water sources is interesting on two counts: first, it restricts women's movements within the *kulhi* since they only visit the water source nearest to their own house; second, since a fixed group of women use the water source, it becomes a place for gathering and conversation. Inadvertently, these interactions contribute to a sense of neighbourhood. At a perceptual level, both these factors have an impact on how women locate/identify themselves as belonging to a particular neighbourhood and what they are (or claim to be) familiar with.

Firewood, or alternative forms of fuel, is another determinant of women's movements, particularly to the forests within or beyond the village. It is a household essential since it is used for cooking twice a day. Women are responsible for both constructing the mud stove in which they cook and for procuring the necessary fuel. Wood is the preferred fuel but it varies in terms of availability because of which other forms of fuel become necessary. In Bhagabondi and Haudah, firewood was gathered from forests in the vicinity of the villages themselves. In Bandudih, the forest lay at a considerable distance from the village and was difficult to access. Consequently, firewood was used together with a range of other fuels. The forests do not belong to the village but are reserved by the state forestry department and villagers have limited access to wood and other forest produce. Further, these forests are not densely wooded, but have young saplings that are periodically planted by the state forestry department under various programmes. In short, the forest is sparse, and villagers have limited legal access, but at the same time, they depend entirely on these wooded tracts for their fuel requirements. Within this context, women strategise how to gather firewood in different ways.

In most cases, villagers head out in the morning between 10:00 am and 12:00 pm to gather wood. When the forest is nearby, children are able to go unaccompanied by adults. During one such visit when I accompanied a group of children, they collected fallen branches and made individual piles. They beat the branches on the ground to remove leaves and stacked the branches in a neat pile. They then pulled off a green branch, stripped its bark and used it to tie their bundle together. They bundled some green leaves and created a soft head support to carry the wood on their head. When all the children were ready with their bundles, they returned home. In villages where the forests are located further away, the process is largely similar with some subtle differences. Here, only women and not children make visits to the forest to gather wood. This is also true for villages where the children regularly attend school and are not available at this time of the day for household chores. The issue of remaining unnoticed is an important concern which the women dealt with by going deep into thickets to chop wood. They chop only a few branches from each thicket so as to leave minimal signs of their work.

This process is severely disrupted when women work as daily wagers since they leave for work as early as 6:00 or 7:00 am in the morning and do not return until about 6:00 pm in the evening. These circumstances have led many villagers to used *gundi*, which is made of small lumps of mud mixed with coal dust. The coal burns but the mud is a filler that delays the process of quickly burning out and gives the women a longer window for cooking. It is however an inefficient fuel and requires separate, specially designed mud stoves. While mud is easily available, coal dust is bought from coal kilns in the vicinity of the village. This requires both money and transport, usually a bicycle. The use of coal dust introduces a different spatial and economic network that has emerged from the constraints faced by women who work as wage labourers. There are also villages such as Bandudih which are located by the side of a busy road and have expanded villages rather than forests in their vicinity. The women here require an entire day, i.e., nearly eight to 10 hours to reach the forest, to gather enough wood and return home. While women do go to the forest when possible, *gundi*, dried leaves and cow dung are all used as fuel depending on availability of firewood. Dried leaves are gathered from the yards around the house and serve as kindling rather than as fuel for cooking an entire meal, while cow dung is pressed into small lumps and used in the stoves. Consumption of cow dung as a fuel, however, affects the plastering of floors since that is also done using the same material. Dried leaves and cow dung are used only under conditions of extreme constraint when nothing else is easily accessible.

In the narratives on the procurement of firewood or other types of fuel, some specific points about women's mobility and engagement with the village and beyond emerge. First, it is apparent that women need to be familiar with the forest areas around the village, but also that they strategise their engagements in light of forest legislation and the fear of running into forest department officials. Second, in the light of the uncertainties with firewood, other networks of interaction and exchange have emerged, such as those with coal-making and -selling establishments. Third, shifts in type of fuel not only entail the procurement of new materials but innovations in ways of using them as well. In most villages, women build two stoves next to one another, one for firewood or cow dung and the other to accommodate *gundi*. Figure 4.1 shows two types of stoves. What is interesting is that the procurement of different forms of fuel appears to be in a constant state of flux, i.e., depending on time, other responsibilities, vagaries such as weather and illness, material availability and economic conditions, women switch between different types of fuel. So the procurement of fuel becomes a complex endeavour, where women need to straddle spatial, material, economic and political variables in order to be able to cook food. These strategies are an important indicator of the complex nature of women's engagements with places and agencies outside the village and form an interesting counterpoint to the idea of their lives being centred on the dwelling. Men spend much of their time outside the house but are rarely involved in these activities. They occasionally cut wood but this is for purposes of construction, repairs involving wood, or for sale. A key difference between men visiting the forest and women doing the same for firewood is that the frequency of women's visits is much higher. Some men may never visit the forest to actually cut wood since construction and repairs are occasional needs and people often turn to commercial timber establishments to buy wood for these purposes. Women, on the other hand, have to routinely visit the forest and therefore negotiate the possibility of encountering forest officials while having to procure enough fuel on a regular basis.

The weekly market is a regional institution through which women encounter other villagers and people from outside the village community. Women frequent the market as this is the place where a range of household items are purchased. Weekly markets are held on different days of the week at fixed places within a locality. While villagers may visit any of the weekly markets in the region, they usually visit the one nearest to their village. Few villages have shops that sell a range of household essentials, so women have to visit the weekly market for vegetables, spices, medicines, cosmetics, tools, and other household miscellany. The weekly market also becomes an important site for women to sell produce from their *barge*, forest produce such as herbs and rice beer. These sales are an important source of women's income, particularly for widows or unmarried women, who either do not own agricultural land or if they do, struggle to cultivate it in the absence of men to assist them.[61] In fact, cultivation and selling of backyard garden produce or the sale of *handia* are often the only options for sustenance in women-headed or women only households. The village market becomes an important point of contact between women and potential buyers for their products. More significantly, given that women's everyday lives are typically spent in and around their dwelling, the *haat* is often the only point of contact with people and things beyond the village.[62] There is a distinction between men's and women's use of village markets. Both men and women frequent the market as sellers. The men who set up stalls are often travelling salesmen by profession and sell things that are bought in urban markets and sold in rural areas, while the women typically come in from surrounding villages to sell vegetables and *handia* (rice beer). As buyers, however, men and women similarly engage with the market since they buy various household essentials such as vegetables. So for women, as both buyers and sellers, the market remains an essential venue for interaction with persons outside the village in order to carry out their various transactions, but for men, it is one of the many sites of interaction with others.

COMPARING MEN'S AND WOMEN'S MOBILITY

In the course of procuring basic necessities such as water, fuel and cow dung women engage with and negotiate various places and entities. These range from meeting forest officials to going to weekly markets, state agencies and commercial establishments such as coal kilns. The pursuit of domestic activities thus expands the range of women's inter-actions with complex networks well beyond the domestic realm. While this appears to contradict my earlier contention that women's lives are centred on the dwelling, it is important to note that all these other places and people that women engage with, lie largely outside of the village community. So even though women become part of complex networks in the course of their domestic responsibilities, these do not significantly impact their inter-personal interactions within the community and in the *kulhi*, where their movements not only remain focused on the domestic realm, but are also limited to the immediate vicinity of their own houses. For men, on the other hand, there is no disjunction between the village and extra-village levels of interaction given that they belong to larger social groups such as the village council.

In and around the house and the *kulhi*, there are subtle thresholds of interaction between women and men from within the village community and people from outside the village. As such, there does not appear to be any restriction in terms of women's movements within dwellings or in the *kulhi*. During my fieldwork days, women and men from the neighbourhood often walked into whichever house I was sketching or taking photographs in and sat around and asked questions while I carried on with the documentation. These interactions typically took place in the courtyards while rooms were usually locked or at least had their entrances covered with curtains. Additionally, women also sit around in the *pide* (plinth alongside the front wall of the house) on the *kulhi racha*, particularly in the afternoons, and chat with each other or with passers-by. Men, on the other hand spend much more time in the *kulhi,* as I mentioned earlier. The *kulhi, racha,* and *barge* are spaces where members of the family and outsiders freely interact with each other. That access is unrestricted is underscored by the fact that women, during the interactions in these spaces, often breastfeed their children wherever they were. The need for privacy or the invisibility of women's bodies is not a major consideration among Santals, and indeed in many Adivasi societies. This is markedly different from many other cultures, where the distinction between interior and exterior spaces, or private and public space, hinges fundamentally on restricted movement and lack of visual connectivity between women and other members of the community. What this also suggests is that the Santals' notions of interiority must be premised on other factors.

Two instances give some insight into what this may be. First, my own patterns of access to different spaces as an outsider, i.e., someone who did not belong to the village community, in the course of field-work and, second, restricted access and other prohibitions around some internal and ritual spaces. While villagers' movements into parts of each other's houses were unrestricted, as I have mentioned earlier, my own access into the houses occurred in distinct phases. When I was first introduced to the villagers, I requested permission to document people's houses and in most cases, I was readily shown around the courtyards. However, if a family was not at home, I was advised to not enter or photograph the courtyard. This occurred when I was walking down the *kulhi* with my guide and attempted to identify the different houses that I may eventually document. In some cases, my guide readily agreed to introduce me to the family, while in others they suggested that the family may not be in the house and so it would be inappropriate for me to enter. I was also advised against photographing such houses even if they were visible from the street by hinting that the family may not approve. In the houses where I did go into the courtyard, the spaces around the courtyard were usually locked or at least had curtains drawn over the entrances. So when I asked to look inside the rooms, I was first shown the animal shelters and then, with a hint of reluctance, the interiors of cooking and sleeping areas. People usually responded that there was nothing worth seeing in the rooms. The restriction on enter-ing the rooms or being able to look inside them was applicable to other villagers who did not belong to the family as well. These rooms did not contain material objects, which was evident from the rooms that I did manage to visit and where only a few things typical of Santal dwellings were to be found. The cooking area, for instance, has a shelf-like structure along one wall, a mud stove with a platform around it, and various pots and pans. They were sites for certain activities such as grain storage, cooking and eating. By restricting access, it was these activities that were being protected from the gaze of people other than immediate family members.

The *bhitar* is the one space within the house that I was never allowed to view or photograph. Scholars of Adivasi societies have noted the fact that only male members of a family are allowed to offer worship within the *bhitar*.[63] Female members of the family prepare the *bhitar* prior to rituals but do not participate in the rituals themselves. Interestingly, this does not include married daughters, who do not enter the *bhitar* in their paternal home, while the husband, the son–in–law in the family, is allowed to do so.[64] This is because a married daughter is considered as part of the husband's clan. The *bhitar* in the parental home houses *bongas* and ancestral spirits of a now–different clan lineage. The *jahira* is another site that has restrictions of access. Only men who own land in the village and are members of the village community are allowed to enter and participate in rituals conducted there, while village women and men from other villages are not. What becomes evident here is that it is the relationship between kinship and ritual locations that structure patterns of access and participation in these spaces. The distinction between interior and exterior spaces is not performed through the gendered body alone, but also through differential access to sacred spaces between family members and other people.

I discussed earlier how the sense of interiority increased in Santal dwellings. It shifted from a distinct dichotomy between inside and outside spaces, to more complex layers of interior space marked by multiple entrances and thresholds in courtyard houses. Compared to the older *kumbha* dwellings, where the interior spaces were used for cooking and for worship and no outsiders were allowed inside, the courtyard dwellings had more gradation. Two thresholds of entrance are perceptible, the first from the *kulhi* into the courtyard and the next from the courtyard into specific rooms. What continued to be common across the transformation is that the *bhitar* remained the least accessible room open only to immediate family members. Both historically and today, it remains the most private part of Santal houses, though the rest of the house has variously opened up to people such as other villagers and complete outsiders. Two arguments may be raised on this basis. First, the persistence of the *bhitar* as the most private space of the house may be attributed to the memory of the *kumbha* and its particular configurations of inside and outside, of an almost sacred centre of the house. Through the various transformations, the *bhitar* has changed, and ranges from a full room to a visually blocked corner of a room depending on the size of the house and family. The principle of limited access on account of sacredness persists. Second, the underpinnings of privacy thresholds in Santal dwellings are primarily varying degrees of access to ritual spaces intersected by taboos around gender. Across various scales of Santal settlements, it is sacred geography that emerges as the more or less continuous principle for spatially structuring inhabitation.

MOBILITY AND PERCEPTION

Even though women's mobility patterns are varied, their lives are inextricably bound to the domestic realm and the dwelling. This seemingly oppositional condition makes sense only when Santal women's awareness about their surroundings is brought into the discussion. During my fieldwork conversations, it appeared that women were not aware, or at least claimed to not be aware of things beyond the domestic sphere. I visited many houses in each village *tola* and asked for permission to document the house and daily lives of the family members. With the hope that people I had met may introduce me to other families, I asked the women about other houses where people were at home during the day and if they would let me document their houses. Women mostly responded that they did not know much about other houses in the village. They explained that they were busy with domestic work during the day and did not have the time to visit other houses. At the same time, they were curious about other houses that I visited. They asked questions such as: how the other houses were kept, what things did people have in the house, and, what did I think of the family? At that time, the questions were surprising given that women did seem to move about the village as they went about their daily chores. Yet, they would offer little or no information about houses or places in other parts of their own *kulhi*.

As my familiarity with some of the village women grew, I realised that women did know a lot about their neighbourhood and quietly shared stories with me. For instance, one family had been ostracised from the village and their house was locked. Towards the end of my fieldwork period, during casual afternoon conversations with two women, I was given two detailed accounts of the feud that led to the family being punished by the village council. Women were not members of the village council and usually heard about these details from their husband, brother, or any other male member of the family. During my previous visits, however, the same women had avoided my questions about that house and had just said that there was no one in the house. Similarly, one woman asked many questions about the headman's wife and said that she did not know her very well. During a later visit, I found that the two women did know each other quite well. During a girl's engagement in the village, the two women were speaking to each other with considerable familiarity and even visited each other's houses. This degree of conversation was however unusual and took place on account of the event because women do not, as such, have many instances of interacting with each other. What emerges here is that women are well aware of their neighbourhood on account of communications that are channelled through the men in a family and occasionally between women themselves. The initial reticence was partly a reaction to my status as an outsider but I realised later that it is also culturally expected that women not know, and therefore be unable to interfere, in matters of other houses and families.

This idea of limited perception is linked to spatial practice because Santals believe that they co-habit this world with spirits and various sites of everyday use in the village are abodes of spirits. Second, Santals have a strong belief in witchcraft and women are particularly susceptible to this, by which it is believed that they may bring harm to others. Women's presence is certain places is not desired since it may displease *bonga* who when angered may cause harm to the villagers.[65] The fear was largely undiscussed but particularly palpable during one fieldwork encounter. I had just been introduced to a man who lived in an old *ath-chala*. On my guide's insistence, he very reluctantly allowed me to enter the verandah of his house. When I asked about the rooms, which were locked, he requested that I don't insist on seeing the room. He feared that if any untoward incident were to occur in the village, he would be blamed for it. While he did not explicitly say so, he was implying that any incident may be attributed to my presence in their house and it may upset the spirits in the house who may then cause harm to the village.

Troisi suggests that 'women are, from time to time, regarded as being imbued with strange mysterious powers,' which gives them the power to cause harm. Women are not born as witches but acquire training from a tutor, usually in secret. The important aspect of witch-craft relevant to this discussion is that witches can cause harm from contact but also from a distance, i.e., through long-range influence, which suggests that physical enclosures of the dwelling may not neces-sarily offer protection against a witch's influence.[66] What they can do is to protect the interiors and the family from the adverse effects of an evil eye or bad omens. Witches are often believed to have an evil eye but may also cause other kinds of harm on account of jealousy or hatred (or any other negative sentiment) towards another person in the village. Considered against a background of women claiming to not know much about other families or houses in the *tola*, it is probable that the belief in the practice of witchcraft is what makes women unwilling to offer information about other houses, since such knowledge about others may be construed as the basis of any mishap that may befall them.

While I argue that the belief in witchcraft appears to limit women's interactions with others and makes them reluctant to discuss their neighbours or the neighbourhood around their *tola*, it is important to note that this was not a subject that any villager was willing to discuss or admit belief in. When I attempted to discuss my limited access to certain spaces such as the *bhitar* or the fact that spaces in Santal houses did not usually have any windows due to beliefs in witchcraft, villagers vaguely denied it. They instead suggested that villagers are often afraid of thieves and so did not prefer to make windows in their houses. Two village elders, in separate places and on occasions mentioned that Santal communities in the past believed in *bhoot-preta* (loosely translated as ghosts and spirits) and so did not build any windows. They did add, however, that such beliefs are in decline, in the sense that many Santals no longer believe in such things. It is impossible to be definitive about the extent to which witchcraft structures Santal lives and environments. What is certain, however, is that women consistently claim to not know much about other families, and incidences of women being accused as witches continue to surface, giving credence to this fear. Newspaper reports every once in a while write about women in particular villages being accused of witchcraft. What can be said beyond doubt is that, this has in the past influenced women's perception of and engagements with their environment, and it continues to do so even today.

In architectural discourses, the physicality and materiality of buildings often makes it difficult to foreground the fluidity of inhabitation. It is easier to operate using dichotomies such as private and public and to directly map these onto social binaries such as gender. In most dwelling environments, and certainly in the case of Santal houses, thresholds of interaction are contingent upon the social actors and practices in question. The logic that animates access and activities in one part of the house may not apply to other areas. For instance, I discussed the *bhitar* as the most inaccessible and private part of Santal houses. Through the lens of religiosity, the Santal dwelling is divided into the *bhitar* as the private realm of the spirits accessible only to men in the family and selected kin, and the rest of the house accessible to all others irrespective of gender. The spaces of cooking and eating are also private activities since Santals nearly never eat and only rarely cook in the open. These spaces, however, have access based on a different logic. Outsiders are not expected to enter during cooking or when the family is eating, for fear of witchcraft or someone causing harm to the family through the food. Access to both these parts of the house is restricted but the rationale for privacy is different.

Epilogue: Whither Adivasi Modernity?

As I finished this manuscript, the Supreme Court of India ordered the 'eviction' of nearly 1,000,000 Adivasi families from forests in 21 states across India. This ruling affects families whose claims to traditional forest lands have been rejected under the Forest Rights Act but against whom the state governments had not yet taken action. The Forest Rights Act was passed in 2006 and gave rights of forest areas within village boundaries to the Adivasis and non-Adivasi forest-dwelling communities. These forests were previously controlled by the State through the forestry department since the time of colonial rule. The Act was a move in the direction of restoring some of the traditional rights to communities. With this ruling, the rights of these families to gather material for their everyday sustenance are legally disrupted. It also signals that Adivasi relationships to the forest, and specifically their impact on the biodiversity of the forest is easily misunderstood.[67] The petition was filed by some wildlife NGOs who claimed that the Forest Rights Acts, which handed back traditional forests to Adivasis and other forest dwelling communities under certain conditions of use, was leading to deforestation. Adivasi groups on the other hand claimed that in many states, their claims were rejected without appropriate cause and require further review. Under these uncertainties, the Supreme Court judgement delivers a hard blow to communities whose very sustenance in most cases depends on access to the forest. This is an important moment to reflect on some of the issues I set out to address in this book. Particularly, I return to the question of how historical invisibility and stereotyping of Adivasi societies continues to lead to dispossession and alienation from their places of living. Surprisingly self-evident as it may appear, the judgement takes a remarkably narrow view of the ways in which the lives of Adivasi communities are meshed with forests. In the past two decades, in spite of the increasing visibility of Adivasi voices, a deeper understanding of Adivasi societies seems to evade popular imagination.

Under these circumstances, what is the ambition of this book? It is assuredly small, but lies in the direction of identifying the ways in which academic scholarship relates to and possibly even shapes popular imagination. One of the starting points is the disciplinary domain in which the project is rooted, viz., architectural history. An important strain that animates architectural history is the relationship between the built environment, people and society. On the one hand is the functional relationship, which is also the more easily investigated one. Buildings offer physical shelter and the spatial configuration of a place corresponds broadly to the social relationships between the inhabitants themselves and between them and the outside world. But places have a deeper significance, which Heidegger described as phenomenologically dwelling, and which many subsequent architectural theorists developed as a significant dimension of architecture.[68] Buildings and places of living create deeply symbolic anchors between people and their environment. They establish relationships between the physical and the metaphysical realms while also, simultaneously, bringing these into existence by virtue of the act of building.[69] Drawing broadly from this philosophical position, this project analysed both sites and processes of dwelling, thus framing architecture as both a noun and a verb. This approach inherently destabilises any fixed idea of tradition. It also de-centres the architectural object as the sole analytical focus and instead locates it alongside the operational logic of the builders and inhabitants. Indigenous built environments are not static, nor bound within fixed social imaginaries of being Santal or Munda or Mahato. What we find instead are ways of building more or less common to a region, intersected by contingencies of time and place that trigger specific developments. As a whole, the architectural landscape is closer to the locality theorised by Appadurai, where each locality is not a bounded entity but one that is cris-crossed by multiple trajectories. Each house and family in Singhbhum presents a particular intersection of historical and contemporary forces. There are commonalities, of course, but to privilege them for the sake of a unified narrative is to deny the differences, and the individual or collective choices that produce them.

When we imagine Adivasi architectural, material or art traditions as being dynamic and in a state of constant flux, it presents a direct challenge, for instance, to heritage narratives which appear to freeze frame certain aspects of Adivasi culture and society, usually in relation to their marketability. This leads to two key problems. First, this representation is often inaccurate since many of the art forms or craft objects do not belong to the communities and places they are associated with. As I discussed in the introduction of this book, Jharkhand has recently witnessed a surge in local handicrafts. While some of the objects (such as those made using *dokra* techniques) and art forms (using the motif of human figures with triangulated bodies or animals painted with dots on brightly coloured surfaces) do clearly have tribal origins, they are non-specifically identified as 'tribal'. Most consumers are not aware of the origins of *dokra* or the particular motifs used in the art work and hence do not recognise the disconnect between geography, community and the art form. The generic association between these objects, practices and Adivasis as an indistinguishable collective, further feeds into the condition of social invisibility. The absence of patronage for local practices or supplanting them with other art or objects, erases the connections between people and the environment, which is materialised through the process of artistic production. In the vein of Heideggerian phenomenology, the art practices or craft objects both produce the connections between people and the environment and also represent them. If the objects and practices change, the connections are irrevocably erased as well. The second problem, of privileging a particular past moment, is of the curatorial kind. If Adivasi art has transformed so much in time, and if, as in the case of Santal domestic art, the use of brushes produces new designs and leads to new aesthetic sensibilities, what moment is truly authentic Adivasi art? By privileging the forest dwelling past, heritage narratives inadvertently frame that as being more authentic than other historical trajectories or contemporary realities. This also renders invisible the complex ways in which Adivasi art has developed through time, which in the case of Singhbhum has been inextricably linked to the engagement with, and therefore, influences of colonial and industrial economies. Some instances of domestic murals that I discussed earlier clearly reference popular visual culture and present a sophisticated rendering of floral and other motifs.

One woman had painted a teddy bear and a dinosaur as part of her mural, which is easily dismissed as a corrupting modern pop culture influence. From the perspective of the art and craft market, this sophistication and experimentation goes against the grain of what is popularly imagined as Adivasi art. From the perspective of the women artists, however, mural art is part of their expression and a canvas for illustrating the motifs they find interesting and worth displaying.

A larger question that this project was concerned with, implicitly though not explicitly, was one of agency in identity and representation. From the perspective of the villagers, there is a clear self-identification as a people who are part of the modern and developed world. Towards the end of my fieldwork visits, I organised a display in the village of the architectural and photographic documentation that I had done. I hoped for some reactions and inputs to the places, objects and my representation of them. I asked the villagers to choose which images they felt were most representational of themselves.[70] While religious places of the *jahira* and *manjhithan* were unanimous first choices, it was the next set which was interesting. In most cases, people chose images of the village school, even if it was not a particularly well-run institution and the local children did not regularly study. To the villagers, the school as an institution represented a way of being modern. As one *manjhi* (headman) pointed out in reference to a picture of a group of girls going to school, 'this picture shows that we are progressive. Our girls go to school regularly, they study. When you tell *bahar ke log* (meaning outsiders), you show them this picture, and tell them Adivasis are not backward. We are developed.' Another elderly villager asserted, '*yeh factory sab hum log hi to banaye hai. Hamara baap-dada log nahi hota, toh kaun banata? Use time par to yahaan aur koi aadmi nahi tha*' (We built these factories. Who would labour on these sites if not for our parents and grandparents? There was nobody else here at that time). The sense of being engaged with contemporary developments at any given moment in time is evidently intrinsic to Adivasi experience today and in the past. Whether it is earning a livelihood in a factory or a quarry or it is painting a teddy bear along more traditional motifs, Adivasi perceptions and engagements with the world are not determined as an imaginary template of 'Adivasi-ness'. They draw from and respond to various conditions just as non-Adivasis do.

While there are multiple ways in which Adivasi voices can be engaged and represented within academic scholarship, the central focus of this project was to foreground the logic of individuals in producing, using, and transforming the built environment. Adivasi habitations as a collective, is constituted without erasing the individual. The narrative that emerges is fragmented and slippery. It doesn't, for instance, give a clear picture of what it means to be Santal. It can, of course, be argued whether such definition is even possible. What is offered is a set of places, practices, perceptions, all of which have transformed and continue to transform under various circumstances. As with much of Adivasi, or indeed any social reality, this is not a narrative that will resolve into a coherent whole, it demands to be engaged with, in all its complexity, if it is not to become a reduced version of itself. Within architectural history discourses, it is quite common to employ the idea of a 'type', which is an abstraction based on certain shared attributes of a complex set of architectural objects. The type often becomes the basis for analysis and theorising and stands in for the whole. The preceding chapters however show that it is nearly impossible to construct a type, though it is possible to identify a range of attributes and their variations. It is also possible to trace conditions under which these variations emerge.

When we centre the logic of individuals, the narrative inherently does not seek out threads of continuity through time. It becomes impossible to essentialise, or even identify sets of places or practices that are central to Adivasi society. The *jahira* is an interesting case. As such, it is historically recognised as the most important institution in Santal society. Santals in every village were unanimous that the *jahira* was the most important site in village life and society. Yet the *jahira* and people's associations to it have not remained unchanged. After the past century and more of settling, contemporary Santal *jahira* show signs of permanence, not in the form of buildings but through elements such as the making of brick and concrete boundary walls, using pre-fabricated concrete posts for the *jahira* shed, and a plinth to commemorate the precise location of worship. Scholars in the past have recorded that the grove was only a cluster of trees. A shed was built and each Sohrai and the *naeke* (priest) would anoint a part of the ground with cow dung before ritual worship.[71] This kind of a sacred site lent itself to frequent movement; each time the community moved to settle in another location, a new site was consecrated. The difference between that setting and the more architecturally defined *jahira* is not just a question of an intangible idea becoming tangible. Neither is it a simple act of making permanent the otherwise transient *jahira*. The very imagination of the place of worship undergoes transformation as the site changes. Scholars note that all men of the community had to participate in the *jahira*, which is understandable considering that the *jahira* was a spiritual anchor for a group that was on the move. Any site of habitation is underpinned by a form of cosmological orientation, and since the group moved from site to site, it had to be re-established each time. The permanent location of the contemporary *jahira* engendered more abstract forms of communities, such as families represented only by their monetary contributions rather than through physical presence. No matter how far beyond the village people travelled, the sacred site was now stabilised in one place and so participation could occur without the physical presence of community members. It may be tempting to reduce this to a form of tokenism and suggest that the *jahira* no longer holds the community together as it did in past. But that would be a premature conclusion since the villagers were unanimous about the *jahira* being the most important institution in the village and representative of Santal culture and society. The point here is that the *jahira* underwent transformation and so did ritual practices and the ways in which communities connect with others through the site.

In a similar vein, by tracing multiple causes and possible effects on multiple sites, a complex narrative of Adivasi history begins to accrue. What gets dismantled in the process is the stereotyping of the Adivasi village as the bounded space of tradition and the city, in contrast, as a bounded site of modernity. Adivasis have historically worked in factories, mines and other industrial sites, while continuing to live in their village settings. They have worked and continue to work as wage labourers in different places and for varying periods but return to their villages for social and ritual commitments. Their domestic lives are lived in the village, or for the urban Adivasi, in the city, but their ritual practices and certain institutions like the *manjhithan* keep alive the memory of a forest dwelling past. Rather than framing these sites as binary opposites of one other, it is useful to imagine them as a continuum of modes of living, composite journeys that comprises an Adivasi individual's life. This also then compels a reimagining of these sites and modes of habitation as belonging entirely to tradition or modernity alone. Neither is the space of the forest or village and all that occurs within its boundary, a traditional practice, nor is all that happens in a city, entirely modern. They are certainly triggers of distinctly different ways of living, considering that each of these sites in and of themselves are complex intersections of the global and the local, and of the diverse social, political, economic, and cultural strands that constitute any habitation. Adivasi subjectivities, rather than belonging to any one space exclusively, are shaped simultaneously by the navigation of these different spaces.

The Supreme Court judgement is an important reminder of the vulnerability of very large numbers of Adivasi communities in contemporary South Asia. Communities have historically transformed but conflict over forest, land, basic resources and contestation of identity have remained a central part of Adivasi life. The focus of this book was not on the epicentres of Adivasi conflict, but most villages and individuals are in the unsettling penumbra of what is a fundamentally conflicted condition. It attempts to substantiate the ordinary as a political project, in order to individualise the past and take it beyond stereotypes that otherwise refuse to go away. It is imperative to fundamentally de-centre singular figures and tropes so that more fluid and diverse stories can emerge. This is imperative given that the simplified labelling of the Adivasi as the 'other' has led to a historically weakened claim to full citizenship.

Notes

1. The advertisement was made by Tata Steel and showed a reenactment of J. N.Tata meeting engineer Julian Kennedy and inviting him to India to build a steel factory. Kennedy was incredulous but realised that J. N. Tata was serious, and eventually did design a number of structures of the initial factory plant.

2. Birsa Munda is one of the most widely known historical adivasi figures from the Chotanagpur region, recognised for organising a campaign against colonial rule. He mobilised adivasis to protest against the agrarian reform which dispossessed adivasis of their land and empowered non-adivasi landlords. He was jailed by the colonial army, where he died at the young age of twenty-five. In the wake of the formation of Jharkhand state, Birsa Munda once again found a strong hold in the public memory of adivasi history. While much has been written about his life in popular and anthropological discourses, Mahasweta's Devi's Bengali novel 'Aranyer Adhikar' ('Jangal ke Davedar' in Hindi) (published in 1979, translated into Hindi with title *Jangal Ke Davedar*) vividly described Birsa Munda's life and struggle.

3. Sinha, Surajit, 'Tribal cultures of peninsular India as a dimension of the little tradition: A preliminary statement,' *Journal of American Folklore* (1958), 504–517.

4. Bandopadhyay, Madhumita, 'Demographic consequences of non-tribal incursion in Chotanagpur region in the colonial period (1850–1950),' *Social Change* 29 (1999), 10–46.

5. Sen, Asoka Kumar. *Redefining Archaeology and the Ethno-History of pre-colonial Singhbhum* in *Indian Folklore Research Journal*, Vol. 7, No. 10 (December 2010).

6. See, for instance, Sahlin, Alex. Personal Impressions of India, January 15th to April 21st 1908. Unpublished Document.

7. Banerjee, Prathama, 'Writing the Adivasi: Some Historiographical Notes,' *Indian Economic and Social History Review*, 53, 1 (2016), 1–23.

8. Bhabhor, Jaswantsinh. Lok Sabha Unstarred Question No. +221, to be Answered on 17.07.2017: Tribal Population. Ministry of Tribal Affairs, Government of India, 2017. Accessed www.indianenvironmentportal.org.in on 18 April 2019.

9. Ibid.

10. Ibid.

11. Somers for instance discusses the position, roles and responsibilities of the headman or *manjhi* in detail. Somers, George, *The Dynamics of Santal Traditions in A Peasant society* (New Delhi: Abhinav Publications, 1977).

12. Beteille, Andre, 'The concept of tribe with special reference to India,' in Chaudhary and Patnaik, *Indian tribes and the mainstream* (New Delhi: Rawat Publications, 2008), 23.

13. *Ibid.*, 34 and Beteille, Andre, *Six essays in comparative sociology* (Delhi: Oxford University Press, 1974), 59.

14. Rycroft, Daniel and Sukanya Das Gupta. *The Politics of belonging in India: Becoming adivasi.* (Abingdon: Routledge, 2011), 1.

15. Beteille, Andre, 'The idea of indigenous people' in *Current Anthropology* (Wenner-Gren Foundation for Anthropological Research, 1998), 187.

16. Archer, W.G, *The hill of flutes: Love, life and poetry in tribal India : A portrait of the Santals.* (Pittsburgh, PA: University of Pittsburgh Press, 1974), 20.

17. I use basic descriptors to indicate social status or relationship rather than women's names in all the chapters. Most Santal women are referred to by their relationship to a male family member or age. So young married women are usually called *bou* (similar to *bahu* which is wife or daughter-in-law in Hindi) while young unmarried girls are called *biti* (similar to *beti* or daughter in Hindi). Older women were mostly referred to as *budi* or old woman. In most cases, women did not know each other's names, or at least did not share the information with me.

18. It is customary among Santal communities for only men to cultivate land. This is possibly linked to the taboos around women digging soil or handling a plough. For further reading on Santal women's contemporary engagement with landownership, agriculture, and other livelihood practices, see Rao, Nitya. Standing One's Ground: Gender, Land and Livelihoods in the Santal Parganas, Jharkhand, India. School of Development Studies, University of East Anglia, Norwich: PhD, University of East Anglia, 2002 and Shah, Alpa. In the shadows of the state: Indigenous politics, environmentalism, and insurgency in Jharkhand. Durham and London: Duke University Press, 2010.

19. The names in this book have been anonymised. However, some of the villages where this study was carried out do feature in a survey map of Singhbhum by Captain Gastrell and De Pree published in 1891.

20. Prof. Digambar Hansdah is a noted Santal scholar, literary figure and activist. He was awarded the Padma Shri in 2018 in recognition of his contribution to Adivasi society.

21. She was referring to the assassination of Indira Gandhi in 1984.

22. Hunter, William Wilson, *Annals of Rural Bengal* (Originally published in 1868. Creative Media Partners LLC, 2015), 205.

23. Bodding, P.O. *How the Santals live* (Calcutta: Royal Asiatic Society of Bengal, 1940), 431–432.

24. *Ibid.*

25. Basu, K.K. 'The History of Singhbhum 1821–1836', *Journal of Bihar Research Society,* 1956: 283–298.

26. Santal geography comprises of regions known as *disom*. Each *disom* comprises a few pir, which in turn is made up of a few villages. While these categories

loosely correspond to present-day administrative regions, they appear to more closely correspond to administrative units in the mid-nineteenth and early twentieth century. They are defined through a mix of collective memory as in the case of western Singhbhum known as Mogulbandi or periods of particular rule as in the case of Seraikela which is known as Singh *disom* after the Singh dynasty of rulers. Personal interview with Prof. Digambar Hansdah.

27. Dalton specifically refers to Ho megalith being found even in places where the community no longer lives. Dalton, E.T. *Descriptive ethnology of Bengal.* Calcutta, 1872, 203.

28. Kanshiram Singh particularly used the word suit to describe a situation where the family felt uncomfortable in a place. The discomfort was linked to the belief in spirits, but he did not say so directly. The inference however is plausible when triangulated with the ways in which Santals and other adivasis associate with places of residence.

29. Damin-i-Koh literally meaning 'skirts of the hills' was an area demarcated by the colonial administration as it sought to bring different parts of the Santal Parganas under control in the early nineteenth century. By reserving the Rajmahal hill areas, the authorities primarily intended to encourage the Paharia adivasis who lived up in the hills to engage in cultivation of the valleys. The Paharias did not take up cultivation and a large number of Santals settled in the region instead. O'Malley, L.S.S., *Bengal District Gazetteers Santal Parganas* (Delhi: Logos Press, 1910), 247–251.

30. For a history of rebel leaders and rebellion in the region, see Mishra, Asha and Chittaranjan Kumar Paty, *Tribal Movements in Jharkhand 1857–2007* (New Delhi: Concept Publishing Company, 2010).

31. In most scholarship on adivasi societies, there is a recurring reference to the concept of *diku* (outsider or foreigner) in reference to people who did not belong to the community. During the nineteenth century, and probably even earlier, *diku* became synonymous with exploitative outsiders who were responsible for the history of adivasi alienation from their traditional home-lands. What I discuss here is how this concept was not an absolute one but became differentiated into different kinds of outsiders, which is identifiable on the basis of thresholds of access into domestic spaces. For a summarised account of the tribal land tenure system and history of alienation through the nineteenth and twentieth centuries, see Ekka, Alex, *Status of Adivasi/ Indigenous Peoples Land Series 4: Jharkhand,* (Delhi: Aakar Books, 2011).

32. For a detailed account of Santal traditions as observed in the late nineneenth and early twentieth century, see Bodding, P.O. *Traditions and Institutions of the Santals* (New Delhi: Gyan Publishing House, 2001 [1916]).

33. Bodding, P.O. *How the Santals Live* (Calcutta: Royal Asiatic Society of Bengal, 1940), 431–432.

34. See Chapter 2 'Tribal Land Tenures' in Ekka, Alex, *Status of Adivasi/Indigenous Peoples Land Series 4: Jharkhand* (Delhi: Aakar Books, 2011), 25–37.

35. Das Gupta, Sukanya, 'Colonial Rule and Agrarian Transition in Singhbhum,' in Das Gupta and Basu, *Narratives from the Margins:Aspects of Adivasi history in India* (Delhi: Primus Books, 2012), 157–158.

36. Das Gupta notes that the Kolhan Government Estate earned rents of ₹64,828 in 1867, and ₹1,77,300 in 1897. The substantial increase was entirely due to the increase in cultivable, and therefore taxable land during this period. There may have been some errors in computation, but the massive increase is evident nonetheless. Ibid.,158–159.

37. O'Malley, L.S.S., *Bengal District Gazetteers Santal Parganas,* (Delhi: Logos Press, 1910), 248.

38. Tuckey, A.D. *Final report on the Survey and Settlement of the Kolhan Government Estate in the District of Singhbhum,* (Calcutta: Bihar and Orissa Department of Land Records and Surveys, 1920), 34–41.

39. While the region has an archaeological history of iron smelting, what I refer to here is modern industrialisation. The mid-nineteenth century topographical map of the area lying to the southwest of present-day Jamshedpur marks the 'Singhbhum Co. Copper Works' in the Asanboni area. Demographic studies by Bandopadhyay also indicated a sharp rise in populations in Chotanagpur on account of industrialisation in this period. Topographical Survey of India, *Chotanagpur Topographical Survey - Portions of Dalbhum and Seraikela,* Sheet No. 7, Scale 1 Mile = 1 Inch (Calcutta, 1874); Bandopadhyay, Madhumita, 'Demographic consequences of non-tribal incursion in Chotanagpur region in the colonial period (1850–1950)' in *Social Change* 29 (1999), 10–46.

40. Bodding, P. O., *How The Santals Live,* (Calcutta: Royal Asiatic Society of Bengal, 1940), 431.

41. Villagers referred to fertilisers as 'sulphates' and pointed out that while the fertilisers helped with better paddy production, it weakened the straw itself and made it unsuitable for roofing.

42. See, for instance, O'Malley, L. S. S., *Bengal District Gazetters: 24 Parganas* (Calcutta: Bengal Secretariat Book Depot, 1914), 67–68.

43. Hunter, William Wilson, *Annals of Rural Bengal,* (Originally published in 1868, Creative Media Partners LLC, 2015), 235–236.

44. Eliade, Mircea, *The sacred and the profane: The nature of religion,* (New York: Harcourt, Brace Jovanovich, c. 1958), 31–32.

45. Huyler, Stephen, *Painted Prayers: Women's Art in Village India* (London: Thames and Hudson, 1994).

46. Hakim, Shaikh Abdul, *Final report on the survey and settlement operations in the Seraikela State, District Singhbhum, 1925–28,* (Patna: The Superintendent, Government Printer, 1953).

47. In a parallel example of art against a backdrop of violence, Munsi discussed Chau, a traditional dance form in Purulia. Munsi, Urmimala Sarkar. 'Many Faces of Purulia: Festivals, Performance, and Extremist Activities' in Elsie Ivancich Dunin and Catherine E. Foley, *Dance, Place, Festival - Proceedings*

of the 27th Symposium of the International Council for Traditional Music. Ireland: University of Limeric, The Irish Academy of Music and Dance, 2014.

48. Imam, 'Kovar and Sohrai Art: The Painted Houses of Hazaribagh' in *Heritage India* 1.4. (2009).

49. Troisi 1979, 28–29.

50. Agricultural land was graded into first, second and third class lands, each of which had decreasing agricultural capacity and therefore varying revenues to be paid to the colonial government for their cultivation. The Survey and Settlement reports produced by the colonial government recorded and formalised this classification and outlined the procedures for classification and subsequent revenue collection. See, for instance, Connolly, *Final report on the survey and settlement operations in the Seraikela Kharswan states, District Singhbhum 1904–1907* (Calcutta: Bengal Secretariat Book Depot, 1908) or Tuckey, *Final report on the survey and settlement of the Kolhan Government Estate in the District of Singhbhum* (Calcutta: Bihar and Orissa Department of Land Records and Surveys, 1920).

51. Bodding, *How the Santals live* (Calcutta: Royal Asiatic Society of Bengal, 1940), 429–430.

52. *Ibid.*, 431.

53. Orans, Martin, 'A Tribal People in An Industrial Setting,' *The Journal of American Folklore* (1958), 84.

54. Sen, Asoka Kumar, 'Redefining Archaeology and the Ethno-History of pre-colonial Singhbhum', *Indian Folklore Research Journal*, Vol. 7, No. 10 (December 2010), 35.

55. Personal interview with Santal scholar Prof. Digambar Hansdah in March 2014.

56. Somers, George, *The dynamics of Santal traditions in a peasant society* (New Delhi: Abhinav Publications, 1977), 243.

57. Troisi, *Tribal religion: Religious beliefs and practices among the Santals,* (Columbia, MO: South Asia Books, 1979), 227.

58. For further reading on traditional governance systems among different Adivasi communities, see Sharan, Singh and Sahu, 'Present status of traditional system of governance among the tribes of Bihar,' *Social change* 29 (1999), 287–301.

59. Golomb, Claire, 'Rudolf Arnheim and the psychology of child art,' *Journal of Aesthetic Education* 27, no. 4 (1993), 14.

60. Troisi, J. *Tribal religion: Religious beliefs and practices among the Santals.* (Columbia, MO.: South Asia Books, 1979), 229.

61. Rao, Nitya. *Standing One's Ground: Gender, Land and Livelihoods in the Santal Parganas, Jharkhand, India* (School of Development Studies, University of East Anglia, Norwich: PhD, University of East Anglia, 2002), 128–129.

62. The scenario is very different for women engaged in wage labour. Given the long hours they spend travelling to sites of work and the different kinds of labour work they typically engage in, their networks and equation with

domestic responsibilities are very different. For ethnographic studies of Adivasi women wage labourers, see Shah 'The labour of love- Seasonal migration from Jharkhand to the brick kilns of other states in India.' *Contributions to Indian Sociology* (2006).

63. Troisi, J. *Tribal religion: Religious beliefs and practices among the Santals* (Columbia, MO: South Asia Books, 1979), 91–92.

64. Ibid.

65. Ibid., 216–224.

66. Ibid., 218–219.

67. scroll.in article titled 'Supreme Court Orders Eviction of More Than Ten Lakh adivasi and Forest Dwelling Families', published on 20 February 2019, accessed on 21 February 2019; TheWire.in titled 'SC Orders Forced Eviction of More Than 1 Million Tribals, Forest-Dwellers' published on 20 February 2019, accessed on 24 February 2019

68. See, for instance, Norberg-Schulz, Christian, *Architecture: Meaning and place- Selected essays* (New York: Electa/ Rizzoli, 1986), *Existence, space and architecture,* (London: Studio Vitsa Limited, 1971), *Genius Loci: Towards a phenomenology of architecture.* New York: Rizzoli, 1980.

69. Heidegger, Martin, '... Poetically Man Dwells...' In *Rethinking Architecture: A Reader in Cultural Theory,* by Neil Leach (Ed.), 109–119. (London, New York: Routledge, 1997).

70. The participatory research encounter is discussed in detail in Bharat, Gauri, 'Their Voice or Mine? Debating People's Agency in the Construction of Adivasi Architectural History,' In Nezar AlSayyad, Mark Gillem, and David Moffat (Eds.), 'Whose Tradition? Discourses in the Built Environment' (London, New York: Routledge, 2017).

71. Troisi, J. *Tribal religion: Religious beliefs and practices among the Santals* (Columbia, MO.: South Asia Books, 1979), 52.

Bibliography

Appadurai, Arjun. 'Introduction: Place and voice in anthropological theory.' *Cultural Anthropology*, 1988: 16–20.

———. 'Putting Hierarchy in its Place.' *Current Anthropology* (Blackwell Publishing) 3, no. 1 (1988a): 36–49.

———. 'The Production of Locality.' In *The Social Life of Things: Commodities in Cultural Perspective*, by Arjun Appadurai 178–199. Cambridge: Cambridge University Press, 1988.

———. 'Theory in Anthropology- Centre and Periphery.' *Comparative studies in society and history* 28, no. 2 (1986): 356–361.

Archer, W.G. *The Hill of Flutes: Love, Life and Poetry in Tribal India : A Portrait of the Santals*. Pittsburgh: University of Pittsburgh Press, 1974.

Areeparampil, Mathew. *Tribals of Jharkhand: Victims of Develoment*. New Delhi: Indian Social Institute, c.1995.

Arnold, Dana, Elvan Altan Ergut, and Belgin Turan Ozkaya. *Rethinking Architectural Historiography*. xx: Routledge, 2006.

Asquith, Lindsay, and Marcel (Eds.) Vellinga. *Vernacular Architecture in the 21st Century: Theory, Education and Practice*. London and New York: Taylor and Francis, 2006.

Bagchi, Amiya Kumar. *Colonialism and the Indian Economy*. New Delhi: Oxford University Press, 2010.

Bandopadhyay, Madhumita. 'Demographic consequences of non-tribal incursion in Chotanagpur region in the colonial period (1850–1950).' *Social Change* 29 (1999): 10–46.

Banerjee, Prathama. 'Culture/ Politics: The Irresolvable Double Bind of the Indian Adivasi.' *Indian Historical Review*, 2006: 99–126.

———. 'Writing the Adivasi - Some Historiographical Notes.' *Indian Economic and Social History Review*, 53, 1, 2016: 1–23. Accessed from https://www.csds.in/uploads/custom_files/1526966373_Writing%20the%20Adivasi.pdf on February 2019.

Basu, K.K. 'The History of Singhbhum 1821–1836.' *Journal of Bihar Research Society*, 1956: 283–298.

Berleant, Arnold. 'The Aesthetic in Place.' In *Constructing Pace: Mind and Matter*, by Sarah Menin (Ed), 41–54. London and New York: Routledge, 2003.

Beteille, Andre. *Six Essays in Comparative Sociology*. Delhi: Oxford University Press, 1974.

Beteille, Andre. 'The concept of tribe with special reference to India.' In *Indian Tribes and the Mainstream*, by Sukant K. Chaudhury and Soumendra Mohan Patnaik, 21–44. New Delhi: Rawat Publications, 2008.

————. 'The Idea of Indigenous People.' *Current Anthropology* (Wenner-Gren Foundation for Anthropological Research), 1998: 187–192.

Bharat, Gauri. 'Their Voice or Mine? Debating People's Agency in the Construction of Adivasi Architectural History.' In Nezar AlSayyad, Mark Gillem, and David Moffat (Eds.), *Whose Tradition? Discourses in the Built Environment*. London, New York: Routledge, 2017.

Bodding, P.O. *How the Santals Live*. Calcutta: Royal Asiatic Society of Bengal, 1940.

————. 'Some remarks on the position of women among the Santals.' *Journal of Bihar and Orissa Research Society*, 1915: 213–28.

————. *Traditions and Institutions of the Santals*. New Delhi: Gyan Publishing House, 2001 (1916).

Bourdier, Jean-Paul, and Nezar AlSayyad. *Dwellings, Settlements and Tradition: Cross Cultural Perspective*. Michigan: University of America Press, 1989.

Buchli, Victor. *An Anthropology of Architecture*. London and New York: Bloomsbury, 2013.

Canter, David. *The Psychology of Place*. London: The Architectural Press Ltd, 1977.

Carrin-Bouez, Marine. *Inner Frontiers: Santal Responses to Acculturation*. Working Paper, Department of Social Science and Development, Chr. Michelsen Institute, Bergen: Chr. Michelsen Institute, Department of Social Science and Development, 1991.

Chakrabarty, Dipesh. 'Epilogue: Reason and the Critique of Historicism.' In *Provincializing Europe: Postcolonial Thought and Historical Difference*, by Dipesh Chakrabarty, 237–255. Princeton, New Jersey: Princeton University Press, 2008.

Chakrabarty, Dipesh. 'Minority Histories, Subaltern Pasts.' *Postcolonial Studies* 1 (1998): 15–29.

Ching, Francis D.K. *Building Construction Illustrated*. New Delhi; New York: Van Nostrand Reinhold, 1975.

Connolly, C.W.E. *Final report on the survey and settlement operations in the Seraikela Kharswan States, District Singhbhum 1904–1907*. Calcutta: Bengal Secretariat Book Depot, 1908.

Corbridge, Stuart. 'Industrial development in tribal India: The case of iron ore mining industry in Singhbhum, Bihar, 1900–1960.' In *Fourth World Dynamics: Jharkhand*, by N. Sengupta. New Delhi: Authors Guild, 1982.

Corbridge, Stuart. 'The Ideology of Tribal Economy and Society: Politics in the Jharkhand 1950–1980.' *Modern Asian Studies* 22 (1) (1988): 1–42.

Corbridge, Stuart, and Sanjay Kumar. 'Community, corruption, landscape: Tales from the tree trade.' In *Jharkhand: Environment, Development, Ethnicity*, by Stuart Corbridge, Sarah Jewitt and Sanjay Kumar, 264–290. New Delhi: Oxford University Press, 2004.

Corbridge, Stuart, and Sarah Jewitt. 'From forest struggles to forest citizens: Joint forest management in the unquiet woods of India's Jharkhand.' In *Jharkhand: Environment, Development, Ethnicity*, by Stuart Corbridge, Sarah Jewitt and Sanjay Kumar, 87–111. New Delhi: Oxford University Press, 2004.

Corbridge, Stuart, Sarah Jewitt, and Sanjay Kumar. *Jharkhand: Environment, Development, Ethnicity*. New Delhi: Oxford University Press, 2004.

Crysler, Greig C. *Writing space- Discourses on Architecture, Urbanism and the Built Environment, 1960–2000*. New York, London: Routledge, 2003.

Dalton, E.T. *Descriptive Ethnology of Bengal*. Calcutta, 1872.

Damodaran, Vinita. 'Customary rights and resistance in the forests of Singhbhum.' In *The politics of belonging in India: Becoming Adivasi*, by Daniel Rycroft and Sangeeta Dasgupta, 103–118. London and New York: Routledge, 2011.

Damodaran, Vinita. 'History, landscape and indigeneity in Chotanagpur, 1850–1980.' *South Asia: Journal for South Asian Studies*, 2007: 77–110.

Damodaran, Vinita. 'Politics of marginality and the construction of indigeneity in Chotanagpur.' *Postcolonial studies: culture, politics, economy* 9 (2) (2006): 179–196.

Dasgupta, Sangeeta, and Raj Sekhar Basu. *Narratives from the Margins: Aspects of Adivasi History in India*. Delhi: Primus Books, 2012.

Datta-Majumder, Nabendu. *The Santal: A Study in Culture Change*. Delhi: Department of Anthropology, Government of India, 1955.

Davidson, J. 'A proposal for the future of vernacular architecture studies.' *ISVS 6- 6th International Seminar on Vernacular Settlements: Contemporary Vernaculars: Places, Processes and Manifestations*. Famagusta, North Cyprus: Eastern Mediterranean University, 2012. 109–122.

de Certeau, Michel. *The practice of everyday life*. Berkeley and Los Angeles: University of California Press, 1988.

Devalle, Susan B.C. *Discourses of Ethnicity: Culture and Protest in Jharkhand*. New Delhi: Sage Publications, 1992.

Devi, Mahasweta. *Jangal ke Davedar* (Hindi translation of Bengali novel 'Aranyer Adhikar'). Delhi: Rajkamal Prakashan, 2008.

Dey, Pradipta. *Sense of Making a Home: A study of Villages in Bolpur in West Bengal*. Unpublished dissertation, Ahmedabad: Faculty of Architecture, CEPT University, 2007.

Dove, Michael, and Carol Carpenter. *Environmental Anthropology: A Historical Reader*. Malden, MA: Blackwell Publishing, 2008.

Dube, Leela. 'Introduction.' In *Visibility and Power: Essays on Women in Society and Development*, by Leela Dube, Eleanor Burke Leacock and Shirley Ardener, xi–xliv. Delhi, Oxford: Oxford University Press, 1986.

Dube, Leela. 'Women's Worlds - Three Encounters.' In *Anthropological Explorations in Gender: Intersecting Fields*, by Leela Dube, 65–85. New Delhi: SAGE Publications, 2001.

Dutta, Gurusadaya. *Folk Arts and Crafts of Bengal – The Collected Papers*. Kolkata: Seagull, 1990.

Dutta, Maya. *Jamshedpur: The growth of the city and its regions*. n.p.: Asiatic Society, 1977.

Edwards, Elizabeth. 'Photographs and History.' In *Museum Materialities: Objects, Engagement, Interpretation*, by Sandra H. Dudley, 21–38. London: Routledge, 2010.

Ekka, Alex. *Status of Adivasi/Indigenous Peoples Land Series - 4: Jharkhand*. Delhi: Aakar Books, 2011.

Eliade, Mircea. *The Sacred and the Profane: The Nature of Religion*. New York: Harcourt, Brace Jovanovich, c. 1958.

Feld, Steven, and Keith H. Basso. *Senses of Place*. Santa Fe, New Mexico: School of American Reseach Press, 1996.

Gastrell, Captain J.E. and G.C. De Pree 'District Singhbhum (Seasons 1859–65).' *Singhbhum, Bihar (District) - Maps*. Calcutta: Survey of India Offices, April 1891.

Glassie, Henry. *Folk Housing in Middle Virginia: A Structural Analysis of Historic Artefacts*. Knoxville: University of Tennessee Press, 1987.

Golomb, Claire. 'Rudolf Arnheim and the psychology of child art.' *Journal of Aesthetic Education* 27, no. 4 (1993): 11–29.

Gupta, Akhil, and James Ferguson. 'Beyond 'Culture': Space, Identity and the Politics of Difference.' *Cultural Anthropology* 7, no. 1 (1992): 6–23.

Gupta, Dipankar. 'Introduction: The certitudes of caste- where identity trumps hierarchy.' *Contributions to Indian Sociology* (Sage Publications), 2004: v-xv.

Haddad, Elie. 'Christian Norberg-Schulz's Phenomenological Project in Architecture.' *Architectural Theory Review*, 2010: 88–101.

Hakim, Shaikh Abdul. *Final Report on the Survey and Settlement Operations in the Seraikela State, District Singhbhum, 1925–28*. Patna: The Superintendent, Government Printer, 1953.

Heidegger, Martin. '... poetically man dwells...' In *Rethinking Architecture: A Reader in Cultural Theory*, by Neil Leach (Ed.), 109–119. London, New York: Routledge, 1997.

Henare, Amiria, Martin Holbraad, and Sari Wastell. 'Introduction: Thinking through things.' In *Thinking Through Things: Theorising Artefacts Ethnographically*, by Amiria Henare, Martin Holbraad and Sari Wastell, 1–31. London: Routledge, 2007.

Hill, Joe. *Contexts, Ideologies and Practices of Small Scale Irrigation Development in East India*. School of Development Studies, University of East Anglia, Norwich: PhD, University of East Anglia, 2008.

Hillier, Bill, and Julienne Hanson. *The Social Logic of Space*. Cambridge: Cambridge University Press, 1984.

Hirsch, Eric, and Michael O'Hanlon. *The Anthropology of Landscape: Perspectives on Place and Space*. Oxford: Clarendon Press, 1995.

Houben, Hugo, and Hubert Guillaud. *Earth Construction: A comprehensive Guide*. NP: Practical Action, 1994.

Hunter, William Wilson. *Annals of Rural Bengal*. Originally published in 1868. Creative Media Partners LLC, 2015.

Huyler, Stephen. *Painted Prayers: Women's Art in Village India*. London: Thames and Hudson, 1994.

Imam, Bulu. 'Khovar and Sohrai Art: The Painted Houses of Hazaribagh' in *Heritage India* 1.4., 2009.

Ingold, Tim. *Being Alive: Essays on Movement, Knowledge and Description*. London and New York: Routledge, 2011.

————. *Making: Anthropology, Archaeology, Art and Architecture*. London and New York: Routledge, 2013.

————. *Redrawing Anthropology*. Farnham, Surrey, England; Burlington, VT., USA: Ashgate Publishing Company, c2011.

————. *The Perception of the Environment: Essays in Livelihood, Dwelling and Skill*. London and New York: Routledge, 2000.

————. 'Towards an ecology of materials.' *Annual Review of Anthropology*, 2012: 427–442.

Kahn, Miriam. 'Your place and mine: Sharing emotional landscapes in Wamira, Papua New Guinea.' In *Senses of Place*, by Steven Feld and Keith H. Basso, 167–196. Santa Fe, New Mexico: School of American Research Press, 1996.

Karan, Pradyumna P. 'Iron mining industry in Singhbhum–Mayurbhanj region of India.' *Economic Geography*, 1957: 349–361.

————. 'Economic Regions of Chota Nagpur, Bihar, India.' *Economic Geography* 29 (3) (1953): 216–250.

Kellett, Peter. 'Living in the field: ethnographic experience of place.' *Architecture Research Quarterly* (Cambridge University Press) 15, no. 04 (December 2011): 341–346.

Kreps, Christina F. 'Museum Balanga as a site of cultural hybridization.' In *Museum Objects: Experiencing the Properties of Things*, by Sandra H. Dudley (Ed), 280–288. London and New York: Routledge, 2012.

Lacey, Walter Graham. *Final report on the revisional survey and settlement operations in Pargana Dalbhum in the district of Singhbhum (1934–38)*. Patna: Superintendent, Government Printing, 1942.

Leach, Andrew. *What is Architectural History*. Cambridge: Polity, 2010.

Lovell, Nadia. 'Wild gods, containing wombs and moving pots: Emplacement and transcience in Watchi belonging.' In *Locality and Belonging*, by Nadia Lovell (Ed), 51–77. London and New York: Routledge, 1998.

Low, Setha M., and Denise Lawrence-Zuniga. 'Introduction: The anthropology of space and place.' In *The Anthropology of Space and Place*, by Setha M., Lawrence-Zuniga, Denise Low, 1–40. Malden, Mass.; Oxford: Blackwell, 2003.

Maharatna, Arup. 'Trends in tribal demography in Jharkhand in the Post-Independence period.' In *Demographic Perspectives on Indian Tribes*, by Arup Maharatna, 188–214. New Delhi: Oxford University Press, 2005.

Mahato, Pashutpati Prasad. *Sanskritization vs. Nirbakization: A study on cultural silence and ethnic memocide in Jharkhand*. Calcutta: Sujan Publications, 2000.

Mann, Harold. *Report of Investigations with Regards to Social Welfare Work at Jamshedpur*. Bombay: The Commercial Press, 1919.

Marchand, Trevor H.J. 'Making knowledge: explorations of the dissoluble relation between minds, bodies, and environment.' *Journal of the Royal Anthropological Institute* 16 (2012): S1–S21.

Mathur, Nita. *Santhal Worldview*. New Delhi: Concept Publishing Company, 2001.

Maudlin, Daniel. *Proceedings of the panel 'Still on the Margin: Reflections on the Perspective of the Canon in Architectural History'* (1st Conference of the European Architectural History Network). Guimaraes, Portugal, 17–20 June 2010.

Miller, Daniel. *Material Cultures: Why Some Things Matter*. London: UCL Press Ltd., 1998.

————. *Stuff*. Cambridge: Polity Press, 2012.

Mishra, Asha and Chittaranjan Kumar Paty. *Tribal Movements in Jharkhand 1857–2007*. New Delhi: Concept Publishing Company 2010.

Moore, Henrietta L. *A Passion for Difference*. Cambridge: Polity Press, 1994.

————. *Space, Text and Gender: An Anthropological Study of the Marakwet in Kenya*. New York: Guilford Press, 1986.

Moutu, Andrew. 'Collecting as a way of being.' In *Thinking Through Things: Theorising Artefacts Ethnographically*, by Amiria Henare, Martin Holbraad and Sari Wastell, 93–112. Abingdon, Oxon.: Routledge, 2007.

Munsi, Urmimala Sarkar. 'Many Faces of Purulia: Festivals, Performance, and Extremist Activities' in Elsie Ivanovich Dunin and Catherine E. Foley, *Dance, Place, Festival* - Proceedings of the 27th Symposium of the International Council for Traditional Music. Ireland: University of Limeric, The Irish Academy of Music and Dance, 2014.

Norberg-Schulz, Christian. *Architecture: Meaning and Place- Selected essays*. New York: Electa/ Rizzoli, 1986.

————. *Existence, Space and Architecture*. London: Studio Vitsa Limited, 1971.

————. *Genius Loci: Towards a Phenomenology of Architecture*. New York: Rizzoli, 1980.

O'Malley, L.S.S. *Bengal District Gazetteers Santal Parganas*. Delhi: Logos Press, 1910.

————. *Bengal District Gazetters - 24 Parganas*. Calcutta: Bengal Secretariat Book Depot, 1914.

Oliver, Paul. *Shelter and Society*. London: Barrie and Rockliff Ltd., 1969.

————. *Shelter in Africa*. London: Barrie and Jenkins, 1971.

Orans, Martin. 'A Tribal People in An Industrial Setting.' *The Journal of American Folklore*, 1958: 422–445.

————. *The Santal: A Tribe in Search of a Great Tradition*. Detriot: Wayne University Press, 1967.

Otero-Pailos, Jorge. *Architecture's Historical Turn: Phenomenology and the Rise of the Postmodern*. Minneapolis: University of Minensota Press, 2010.

Pink, Sarah. *Doing Visual Ethnography*. London, Thousand Oaks, New Delhi: Sage Publications, 2001.

————. *Situating Everyday Life*. London, Thousand Oaks, CA: Sage, 2012.

Quinn, Naomi. 'Anthropological studies on women's status.' *Annual Review of Anthropology*, 1977: 181–225.

Rao, Nitya. *Standing One's Ground: Gender, Land and Livelihoods in the Santal Parganas, Jharkhand, India*. School of Development Studies, University of East Anglia, Norwich: PhD, University of East Anglia, 2002.

Rapoport, Amos. *House Form and Culture*. Englewoods Cliffs, NJ: Prentice Hall, 1969.

————. *Meaning in the Built Environment: A Nonverbal Communication Approach*. California, New York: Sage Publications, 1982.

Reid, J. *Final report on the survey and settlement of Pargana Dalbhum in Singhbhum 1906 to 1911*. Calcutta: Bihar and Orissa Board of Revenue, 1913.

Rudofsky, Bernard. *Architecture without Architects*. New York: Museum of Moden Art, 1964.

Rycroft, Daniel. 'Born from the soil: The indigenous mural aesthetic of Kheroals in Jharkhand, Eastern India.' *South Asian Studies*, 1996: 67–81.

Rycroft, Daniel J., and Sangeeta Dasgupta. *The Politics of Belonging in India: Becoming Adivasi*. Abingdon: Routledge, 2011.

Sahlin, Alex. Personal Impressions of India—January 15th to April 21st 1908. Unpublished Document.

Schodek, Daniel L. *Structures (Ed.4)*. New Delhi: Prentice Hall Inc., 2002.

Seamon, David. *A Geography of the Lifeworld- Movement, Rest and Encounter*. London: Croon Helm, 1979.

Seamon, David, and Robert Mugerauer. *Dwelling, Place and Environment*. Malabar, Florida: Kreiger Publishing Company, 2000.

Sen, Asoka Kumar. *Redefining Archaeology and the Ethno-History of pre-colonial Singhbhum*. Indian Folklore Research Journal, Vol. 7, No. 10, December 2010.

Sengupta, Shyamalkanti. *Perception of Folk Environments*. New Delhi, 2003.

Shah, Alpa. *In the Shadows of the State: Indigenous Politics, Environmentalism, and Insurgency in Jharkhand*. Durham and London: Duke University Press, 2010.

————. 'The labour of love- Seasonal migration from Jharkhand to the brick kilns of other states in India.' *Contributions to Indian Sociology*, 2006: 91–118.

Shah, Dhaval. *Comparison of Santal and Bhumij houses*. Unpublished dissertation, Ahmedabad: Faculty of Architecture, CEPT University, 2009.

Shahshahani, Soheila. 'Women whisper, men kill: A case study of the Mamasani pastoral nomads of Iran.' In *Visibility and Power: Essays on Women in Society and Development*, by Leela Dube, Eleanor Burke Leacock and Shirley Ardner, 85–97. Delhi, Oxford: Oxford University Press, 1986.

Sharan, Ramesh, Harishwar Dayal, and Promod Kumar Sinha. 'Socio-economic situation of the tribals in the Jharkhand region of Bihar.' *Social Change* 29 (1999): 244–276.

Sharan, Ramesh, Prabhat K Singh, and Suresh P Sahu. 'Present status of traditional system of governance among the tribes of Bihar.' *Social Change* 29 (1999): 287–301.

Sharma, Suresh. *Tribal Identity and the Modern World*. New Delhi/ Thousand Oaks/ London: SAGE Publications and United Nations University Press, 1994.

Sinha, Surajit. 'Tribal cultures of peninsular India as a dimension of the little tradition: A preliminary statement.' *Journal of American Folklore*, 1958: 504–517.

Skaria, Ajay. *Hybrid Histories: Forests, Frontiers and Wildness in Western India*. Delhi:
Oxford University Press, 1999.

Smith, David Woodruff. *Husserl*. London: Routledge, 2007.

Somers, George. *The Dynamics of Santal Traditions in a Peasant Society*. New Delhi:
Abhinav Publications, 1977.

Tilley, Christopher. *A Phenomenology of Landscape: Places, Paths and Monuments*.
Oxford: Berg Publishers, 1994.

Troisi, J. *Tribal Religion: Religious Beliefs and Practices among the Santals*. Columbia,
MO.: South Asia Books, 1979.

Tuckey, A.D. *Final report on the survey and settlement of the Kolhan Government Estate
in the District of Singhbhum*. Calcutta: Bihar and Orissa Department of Land
Records and Surveys, 1920.

Vidyarthi, L.P. *Socio-cultural implications of industrialisation in India- Case study of tribal
Bihar*. New Delhi: Research Program Committee, 1970.

———. *Ghagra: A Village in Chotanagpur*. New Delhi: Office of the Registrar
General, India: Ministry of Home Affairs, 1966.

Visweswaran, Kamala. *Fictions of Feminist Ethnography*. Minneapolis, London:
University of Minnesota Press, 1994.

Wilmsen, Edwin N. *Land Filled with Flies: A Political Economy of the Kalahari*.
Chicago, London: The University of Chicago Press, 1989.

Zwerger, Klaus. *Wood and Wood Joints: Building Traditions of Europe and Japan*. Basel;
Berlin; Boston: Birkhauser, 1997.

Index

About the Author

Gauri Bharat is Associate Professor, Faculty of Architecture, and Program Chair of Architectural History and Theory at CEPT University, Ahmedabad. Her research interests include understanding how people engage with the built environments, and the ways in which people produce, transform and inhabit them. She combines her knowledge of art history, from PhD at the University of East Anglia, with her understanding of architecture, from MA Arch. from National University of Singapore, for her work on Adivasi-built environments as an archive of history.

A major share of India's population is in its prime and of working age. However, with the gaping inequalities in our society, the youth encounter gross disparities in their life chances and opportunities to realise their potential. This book highlights the social, economic and political challenges that shackle India's young population. It argues for recognition of the intertwining of the social and the economic factors, searches for answers beyond the reigning paradigm of 'growth' and envisages a more just and equal society.

An analysis of India's demographic transition and why the 'youth bulge' has not meant better jobs for the youth.

For special offers on this and other books from SAGE, write to marketing@sagepub.in

Explore our range at
www.sagepub.in

Hardback
9789353288020

Written by psychologists and others using a psychosocial lens, *Surviving on the Edge* looks at family, gender, disability and ethnicity in order to better understand prejudice and social violence. The book includes a range of essays—theoretical, narrative accounts and case studies—which question established assumptions as to how violence relates to categories of gender, family, disability and trauma. It also considers the impacts of social violence and possible interventions to address trauma at both the individual and collective levels.

This book discusses the range of prejudice and violence in our society, their traumatic impacts and ideas for transformation.

For special offers on this and other books from SAGE, write to marketing@sagepub.in

Explore our range at
www.sagepub.in

Hardback
9789353283148

Against All Odds uses vivid ethnographic narratives to study linkages between socio-economic conditions and the mental health of women living in low-income neighbourhoods of big cities. The author illustrates how the social position of women and factors inherent in urbanism have an impact on the level of psychosocial distress they experience. The book also takes stock of the different kinds of local 'healing' processes sought by women, and examines how the women's movement and cultural ways of healing have helped women in reducing the distress and violence in their everyday lives.

An in-depth study of the psychosocial distress a big city creates for and in women.

For special offers on this and other books from SAGE, write to marketing@sagepub.in

Explore our range at
www.sagepub.in

Hardback
9789353281915

A first of its kind, this volume provides a series of case studies from South Asia that detail the quest for justice, the links that can be drawn from different countries in the region and the points of contact and divergences in the enunciation and practice of law. The book looks at South Asia as a region bound together through war and collective violence. A second theme that runs through the book discusses the corrosive and affective power of violence in its ability to forge new solidary groups and communities.

A look at how justice has been denied in various parts of South Asia—India, Pakistan, Bangladesh, Sri Lanka, Nepal.

For special offers on this and other books from SAGE, write to marketing@sagepub.in

Explore our range at
www.sagepub.in

Hardback
9789352806539